On The Journey...
Home

On The Journey... Home

**Based on the true story of Pastor
Duane and Gretchen Pippitt**

Susan Free

ON THE JOURNEY…HOME

Cover Photo: http://www.alamy.com - Image ID C8F2K9 (Eastern Oregon, Burns)

Front/Back Cover: Design by Chris Fechter
Website Design and Social Media Director – Michelle Wittel
Website: http://www.freetheheartministries.com
Email: freetheheartministries@gmail.com

Interior Layout Design: Amnet Systems

Dedication

This book is dedicated to Pastor Duane & Gretchen Pippitt.
We thank you for your forty-one years of service to the church by
teaching *us about the love of Jesus,*
living *as an example for all of us to watch, and*
sharing *your trials and love with us.*
May God bless your days as you continue to serve the Lord.

A portion of the net proceeds of this book will be dedicated to Camp Scholarships in Memory of Taylor Pippett, Fellowship of Montgomery, 12681 FM 149, Montgomery, Texas 77316

Trust in the Lord with all your heart;
And lean not on your own understanding.
In all your ways acknowledge Him,
and He shall direct your paths.
Proverbs 3:5-6 (NKJV)

Table of Contents

Acknowledgements · ix

Introduction · xi

Chapter 1 Thank You Redmond Assembly of God · · · · · · · · · · · · · · · 1

Chapter 2 The Journey Begins · 5

Chapter 3 Ministry Life and Leukemia Trials · · · · · · · · · · · · · · ·15

Chapter 4 Unbelievable Grief ·21

Chapter 5 Retirement Plans ·33

Chapter 6 Thank You to Our Staff ·39

Chapter 7 Saying Good-Bye · 44

SERMONS ·57

Chapter 8 A Firm Foundation ·59

Chapter 9 Commitment To God · 68

Chapter 10 Pursuing God · 80

Chapter 11 Understanding Contentment · · · · · · · · · · · · · · · · · ·88

Chapter 12 The Golden Rule ·93

Chapter 13 Facing Impossible Situations · · · · · · · · · · · · · · · ·101

Chapter 14 Cultivating Thankfulness · · · · · · · · · · · · · · · · · ·111

Chapter 15 Easter – Life Changing · · · · · · · · · · · · · · · · · · ·117

Chapter 16 Understanding Communion · · · · · · · · · · · · · · · · · ·126

Chapter 17 Mother's Day - Empowering with Encouragement · · · · · · ·134

Chapter 18 Father's Day Message ·141

Chapter 19 Importance of Missions · · · · · · · · · · · · · · · · · · ·149

Chapter 20 Christmas Story of Salvation · · · · · · · · · · · · · · · ·157

Chapter 21 A Heavenly Place ·162

Chapter 22 On The Journey Home ·168

Lord's Prayer ·177

Celebrate Recovery ·179

End Notes ·181

About the Author ·185

Acknowledgements

I THANK GOD, JESUS, AND the Holy Spirit for bringing me into the life of Pastor Duane and his gracious wife, Gretchen, at the Redmond Assembly of God. In 2020, my husband, Bob, and our close friends, Jerry and Donna Kelly, began attending and each moment has been a true blessing in our walk with the Lord.

This book, *On The Journey…Home* would not be possible without Pastor Duane and Gretchen's willingness to humbly share their journey from childhood through their forty-one years of ministry. Thank you for trusting me with your love story, your journey through the ministry, and your struggles of fourteen years with chronic lymphocytic leukemia as you continued to serve the Lord. As you shared the excruciating loss of your granddaughter during the summer of 2023, I can still feel my heart hurting; words are not enough to express my sorrow for your unfortunate loss.

God nudged my heart to write this story as Pastor Duane spoke of his grief and asked God, Why? God Why? A pastor who has served God all his life expresses his tender cries to the Lord. Why, a child, I don't understand? This is a road he has never been on. He knows God's promises, yet he hurts and cries and understands he needs to lean on Jesus. His realness and honesty teach us that the Lord is by our side no matter how hard it gets. Some times are harder than others. Pastor says, "With tears, we praise Him, sing to Him, and lean on Him, even though we don't understand the whys." These words inspire us to trust Jesus and keep Him close as we struggle through the trials of life.

I thank all members of the congregation who took the time to write beautiful words of love and respect to Pastor and Gretchen as they begin retirement. I especially thank the other pastors and staff who worked alongside Pastor Duane and Gretchen for years. As you read their words, you will see that Pastor Duane wasn't just a pastor but a genuine "mentor" who encouraged those around him to excel and be the best they could be. Pastor and Gretchen united everyone as family, loving and supporting them.

With God's love, I thank my husband, Bob, for sharing his time with me as I sat in my quiet office tapping on the laptop all hours of the night. I give a special thank you to my friend, Donna, who is my greatest encourager to keep going, even when times get tough. My brainy daughter, Michelle, helped me limp through the techy world of websites and social media. I couldn't have done it without her. Thank you to my graphic artist friend, Chris Fechter, who always makes beautiful book covers out of my hen-scratch. Thank you to my dear friends, Mike and Belinda West and Johnny and Debbie McDaniel, who prayed at our bible studies. You all mean the world to me.

I thank God from the bottom of my heart. I start each writing session with prayer thanking Him for what He has done as I quietly listen for His words. Do not be anxious about anything; instead, pray about everything. Please fill me with your peace and strength as I trust in your unfailing love. You are with me always. Amen.

Introduction

THIS BOOK IS CALLED ***On the Journey…Home***. What does it mean to journey home? Some may picture the home they grew up in, with brothers and sisters, pets, school, and friends. Perhaps it is a cozy memory of a place where you still like to travel home to while visiting parents or relatives.

Other people may have a vision of a chaotic home where parents argued and fought with each other, where there was strife, alcoholism, physical or sexual abuse, shortage of food, or only one parent present. Perhaps you had parents who had to work, leaving you to be a latch-key kid where you were alone after school with no supervision. Unfortunately, there are those who had no real home at all, moved around from place to place, lived in a car, placed in a relative's or foster-care home, or given up for adoption, or even neglected or abused.

The real definition of '**home**' is a rooted foundation of loving hearts and souls connected to a place called home. It is not just a building or a room, but a place where love dwells. Typically, we classify home as where we were raised as a child. A home can be classified as a ranch, farm, apartment, suburban home, condo, a motorhome, cabin, cottage, a camper, a mansion, a homestead, or a shelter. We all have a tendency to define home differently, depending on the circumstances and happiness of the home.

As adults, we strive to make our own home the core of where not just your heart is, but the hearts of those we love and trust. We may have spouses, children, and other family members living there. This is why most homes have photos on the wall or end table to show the hearts and faces of the people that are welcome in their home. The fact still remains that the hearts that enter your doorway are what truly defines it as home. We hear phrases of "our home is our castle", home sweet home", "home free", "back home", "my hometown", or "headed home".

Yet, there is another beautiful definition of home and that is "Jesus calling us home". He has made a place for us, as believers, and when we are called home to be with Jesus, it will be the best place to call **home** for eternity. The Bible states in John 14:3, "And if I go and prepare a place for you, I will come back and take you to be with me that you also may be where I am" (NIV).

This book called **On the Journey...Home** is a book based on the true story of Pastor Duane and Gretchen Pippitt, sharing their life journey meeting as teenagers, joining in marriage, raising children, all while serving the Lord for forty-one years in the ministry. This journey may sound like a fairy tale, but it is far from it. They show us through battling leukemia for fourteen years, losing parents, best friends, and close members of the congregation that the trials of life are real. Being a pastor and the wife of a pastor does not mean life is always fair and just.

When their fourteen-year-old granddaughter unexpectedly dies in an accident, they show us how to be vulnerable, stay close to Jesus and trust in Him for everything. Each day is significant as they show us their grief, pain, and suffering. They show us how to breathe through the trials of life and it is only with Jesus that we receive enough strength and comfort to keep moving forward.

Pastor Duane's call to the ministry maintains a pure and simple devotion to Jesus and His Word. His ministerial gift has specific abilities to feed, lead, and love his flock by humbly loving God. His wife, Gretchen, shows her graceful strength in loving the Lord by spreading that love to members of the congregation, quietly teaching and serving behind the scenes, as she supports her husband and her church.

One characteristic of a good pastor is that his faith in Christ must first be 'real'. His tested Christian experience is transparent and shared with his congregation for learning, steadfast faith and a growing sense of humbling grace. Pastor Duane's call to the ministry shows us his character, his faithfulness to God through the written Word, his sensitivity to other's needs, his ability to speak the truth to sinners, his humor, and his vulnerability to show his realness through adversity.

As you read this book, you will experience the love Pastor Duane and Gretchen have for each other, our congregation, and for our Lord. You will also experience the genuine love the congregation has for them.

Join us, as we travel ***"On the Journey…Home"*** with Duane and Gretchen Pippitt, and learn what God can do in the lives of ordinary people who love and follow the Lord.

Susan Free – Writer

CHAPTER 1

Thank You Redmond Assembly of God

IN JANUARY OF 2024, PASTOR Duane and Gretchen Pippitt gathered on the stage after ending the Sunday sermon on commitment.

As the closing prayer ended, the congregation couldn't help noticing that the Pastor's voice appeared breathless and anxious. His wife, Gretchen, is standing slightly behind him as if to support him as the words follow:

Pastor Duane clears his throat and begins speaking, "As you know, a few times over the years, I have had what I call family talks with you, and again, this morning is one of those times."

Gretchen and I would like to have a family talk this morning. Gretchen and I have had the greatest joy of serving this church for twenty-two years after serving forty-one years in ministry. We have baptized our children and grandchildren here at Redmond Assembly of God. We have married our children here. We have baptized and married your children and grandchildren here. We have lost and buried family members here.

We have been through my leukemia treatments for eleven years. Pastor hesitates and looks down for a few seconds and, with a crackly voice, says, "Last year, we lost our young teenage granddaughter in Texas to an unfortunate accident, and we as a family continue to grieve. This year has been difficult for our family. We have cried, laughed, and talked together through all the ups and downs of life."

That said, I want to reiterate that it has been our greatest joy, privilege, and honor to serve this wonderful family we call Redmond Assembly of God! This morning, I want to share with you that I will be retiring effective August 31st of this year. Over the past several months, through prayer and quiet time before the Lord, He has made it clear that it is time to pass the baton.

God has blessed us with the most remarkable church family, board, staff, and ministry leaders anyone could ever ask for or hope for. As I stand here shaking and crying inside, I want to thank each of you from the bottom of my heart. Please hear my heart. I love this church family, and I'm not leaving for a few more months, so we have plenty of time to navigate this change. You are in good hands with a very loving church board God has given you. I believe God's timing is perfect, and this is the time.

So, I want to encourage you to pray and not ask many questions that we don't have answers to yet. Gretchen and I are retiring as your Pastors. I'm not going anywhere else to pastor a different church, and we are not moving out of Oregon. We plan to stay in Central Oregon and live on our little farm.

Where do we go from here? Moving forward, I won't be involved in any future decisions regarding selecting a new pastor. This decision will be the responsibility of the church board as they work closely with the OMN (Oregon Ministry Network) of Assembly of God to implement a smooth transition to a new pastor. So let's walk slowly through this process, have faith in this new season for all of us, and stay faithful in the Lord's business of leading people into a relationship with Jesus Christ and seeing their lives changed forever. We absolutely love this church and we love you!

As Pastor Duane and Gretchen look into each other's tearful eyes, knowing this announcement is a big one for the church and a big step for them as they prepare to retire; they feel almost a sigh of relief knowing they had finally made the announcement after so many months of prayer and discussion. The congregation is shocked at hearing the news. Some people react immediately with sadness and quiet tears, while others congratulate them on the news and encourage them as they follow the Lord.

In the days ahead, people respond in various ways by talking, texting, emailing, or sending a card about how much they will miss them. The response is overwhelming, and Pastor Duane has private thoughts, *"Are we doing the right thing?" "Lord, is this the right time?"* The overwhelming response gives us pause to begin to doubt our decision, yet we stay reminded to follow the Lord's nudges and leave everything at the foot of the cross.

Change is so hard on people in general. We sometimes react poorly to change. It means we have to adjust our lives once again, and this creates anxiety. Even when the Lord calls us to a different season of our lives or puts us in a different mission field, we can sometimes get anxious about the "unknown." Will I like it? Will I miss my old routine?

As people, when our cell phone loses its' charge in the middle of a busy day, our car battery goes dead in the Safeway parking lot, or the dishwasher quits working the day before the company arrives, our response is usually not favorable. When we receive an unfavorable medical diagnosis, or we decide to leave our career or retire, or we lose a loved one, our world once again changes. We have learned through Jesus that if we stay close to Him and trust Him with our hearts, He leads us through the trials in a gentle and loving manner.

We are creatures of habit, and change can be difficult--as if the mind is on a constant battlefield. As life progresses, change is inevitable for everyone, yet we can count on the Holy Spirit being with us as we move ahead with grace to follow Jesus.

In past sermons, Pastor Duane has talked about one of his favorite scriptures and what a great God we serve, quoting Proverbs 3:5-6, *"Trust in the Lord with all your heart; and lean not on your own understanding. In all your ways acknowledge Him, and He shall direct your paths"*(NKJV). In other words, we need to trust the Lord we serve with everything and not try to figure it out ourselves. We can't run ahead of God's plans for us. We must seek His will, and He will show us which road to take throughout our entire life.

Pastor Duane states, "God has been there, even when I doubted Him or asked, "Why God? He has led me, and He is still leading me through fire, anxiety, depression, great sadness, loss, and self-doubt. I am a daily work in progress, and I am still "On the Journey...Home" to one day, like all of us, meeting our precious Jesus in heaven."

One day, the words I long to hear from Jesus are, *"Well done, my good and faithful servant. You have been faithful in handling this small amount, so now I will give you many more responsibilities. Let's celebrate together!"*(Matthew 25:23)

♡ **Jim and Carolyn Mitchell**: Pastor Duane and Gretchen, we *thank God for the years of service you have given to our church family and our personal family all these years at Redmond Assembly of God. We thank God for a pastor who teaches God's Word, the Bible; not only teaching it, but living it.*

We know as you enter this new season in your life of retirement, God is going to continually bless you and use you for His work. Retirement is not an end to your ministry God has put on your life, but a new chapter and adventure. We pray God's many blessings on your life as your enter this new season.

Love and Prayers, Jim & Carolyn Mitchell

♡ **Dan and Linda Jackson**: *Thank you, Pastor Duane and Gretchen, for twenty-two years of love and caring. Your commitment to Redmond Assembly has made permanent changes in many lives, and only eternity will reveal the full extent of those changes. You will be missed more than you will ever know. Thank you for trusting us to teach God's word. We have truly been blessed more than the students in our class. Thank you for loving our children, grand-children and great grand-children. You have both been shining examples and we are eternally grateful. May God fill your hearts and lives with all you are dreaming about in retirement. Thanks again! Dan & Linda Jackson*

CHAPTER 2

The Journey Begins

WHEN ASKED ABOUT THEIR CHILDHOOD history, Duane stated, "I was born at the Air Force Hospital near Portland International Airport on September 23, 1959. My family always joked around that I was born at the airport. I was raised in Alfalfa, Oregon, on a twenty-acre farm, helping my parents raise horses, cattle, and pigs while putting up hay—all while attending elementary school in Alfalfa. During fifth and sixth grade, I attended grade school in Redmond and then middle and high school in Bend. In those days, Bend High School was the only high school."

Gretchen states, "I was born in Roseburg, Oregon on a hot summer day on August 2, 1962. My family lived in Myrtle Creek, a small town west of Roseburg. When I was two years old, my family moved to Bend, where I lived until my sophomore year in high school. Both of my parents worked for the school district, and they had summers off, so we traveled and camped all over Oregon. When they divorced, my dad moved out of the house, but he was still the principal of my school, so I got to see him every day. That was nice. Eventually, my dad moved to Alaska, where I saw him only twice a year, during the summer and Christmas. I found this time in life difficult. We were very close and I missed having my dad around.

A few years later, my mom remarried a man she met at Parents without Partners, and we moved to Salem for the last two years of my high school years. He was very charismatic and funny—the life of the party. Yet when my stepdad was drinking and everyone left, he became loud, screaming at us, and started abusing my mom by hitting and beating her. It was difficult watching my mom get mistreated, and it made me angry.

Most people don't know this about me, but while I attended McNary High School in Salem, I planned to go to law school and become an advocate for women's rights. Even though my law school plans changed, I have always had a passion for gathering young women together to help them grow in their confidence, help them realize how valuable they are to God, while learning to walk with the Lord through their difficult situations.

I had other interests growing up that some people may not know about me. As a kid, I learned from my dad how to tie my own flies for fly fishing, shoot a black-powdered rifle, and hunt upland game birds. Later in life, I dappled in bird taxidermy for five years. The first bird I killed and stuffed was a 'chukar.' We laughed because when I stuffed it, I accidentally bent the knees outward instead of inward from the body and I couldn't figure out why it looked so strange. I also stuffed a wood duck, some quail, and a few other birds.

One funny moment was when I walked into the house to find out my schnauzer dog had shredded the chukar bird to bits and had feathers every-where. I laughed, imagining the battle between my dog and a stuffed bird. I think he won!"

When asked about his childhood, Pastor Duane stated, "I grew up in the Assembly of God church in Bend, Oregon. My mom was a loyal believer in Christ Jesus and taught my sister, Cindy, and me all about Jesus. My parents grew up and married in Brush, Colorado. My dad, Del, served in the Air Force from 1954 to 1963 and deployed to North Africa during the Cuban Missile Crisis, so he was away in the military during most of my first three years of life.

In the military, something changed for him, and he stepped away from the faith. Dad worked two jobs, working hard to earn a living for the family. My mom took us to church every Sunday, and she set some strict rules on what we could and could not do. We were not allowed to play cards, dance, or participate in any drinking or smoking.

Our church was rigid, and it felt like we would go to hell for everything we did wrong. While I was growing up, Dad did not attend church with us, but later on in life, he found Jesus and dedicated his life to Him. My mom also worked during the week, so when Sunday afternoons rolled around after church, I would go to my grandpa and grandma's house to stay the week with them until Friday.

My young years with my grandparents stay etched in my mind as a happy place where I felt loved and cared for while witnessing their love for Jesus. My grandparents were faithful Christians. My grandma was a great cook, washed clothes with the old wringer-washing machine, and always wore an apron and cat-like eyeglasses. She fixed the same breakfast of one-half of a grapefruit, two poached eggs, and two pieces of burnt toast every morning. After breakfast, they would pray and read from the Bible. I was impressed watching them love the Lord. Grandma was always loving and comfortable to be around, and to this day, I still love burnt toast and treasure fond loving memories of her.

I have great boyhood memories of my grandpa talking to the cows in the barn, going to the Madras livestock auction on Thursdays, and riding around in his 1957 Plymouth station wagon as he worked as a "ditch rider." He drove around wearing his bib overalls, measuring the water taken from the canal for each farm. Sometimes, neighbors had incidents where one farmer would steal another farmer's water. My grandpa's work of measuring the water helped deter the farmers from stealing water from each other. Grandpa had a rule: Do not touch my #4 pencils.

Grandpa's second rule was to not lean on the 1957 Plymouth's passenger door as he drove, as the door was broken, and it would fly open. On one particular day, I was leaning on the door, as kids do, and as he drove faster than expected out of the driveway, the door flew open, and I tumbled out into the ditch. It all happened so fast; he quickly stopped the vehicle and ran to where I was lying in the ditch to see if I was all right. Once he saw that I was not injured, he became upset that I had disobeyed him by leaning on the door. He then proceeded to spank me for not doing as I was told. It didn't bother me because I knew he loved me.

He was a great male figure during my growing-up years. I was a sophomore in high school when my grandpa died. He was visiting my aunt and went to lift the heavy suitcases into the trunk of the car, and he fell over and died instantly, shocking all of us. Losing him was a significant loss in my life, and to this day, I still miss him. I loved him so much. Ironically, he died the same Memorial Day weekend that I met Gretchen. When he died, it really shook my faith and I checked out from the church. For six years, I attended church but was more interested in having fun with my friends without all the rules and restrictions.

In my junior year of high school, one of my friends and I started dappling in some alcohol. We would load up the car with beer, one-half gallon of milk, a box of Captain Crunch, and a bag of Doritos (that is all we could afford) and head to Prineville Reservoir or Cultus Lake, located off the High Lakes Highway of Bend. We hung out at the lakes, swimming and acting like typical, cool teenage boys, drinking beer and eating our Doritos. I rebelled from everything I had learned, but Jesus soon had other ideas.

Many people may not know that I grew up with cowboys, my dad being one of them, learning to team rope steers (I roped the head of the steer while my teammate roped the hind legs). I also participated in the peewee rodeo as a youngster. I joined the roping club and participated in what they called jackpot roping.

In team roping, two cowboys work together to rope a steer. One cowboy, the header, goes first and ropes the steer's horns. The other cowboy, the heeler, follows behind and ropes the steer's hind legs. The two cowboys work together to stop the steer.

Jackpot roping aims to rope the steer as quickly as possible. The professional team with the fastest time wins eighty percent of the jackpot 'payout' money from entry fees. The other twenty percent of winnings are divided between second and third-place teams. We weren't very professional; we just threw money into a hat and enjoyed the fun. I loved my roping days. My dad had a bumper sticker on his old pickup that read "I'm a Roper, Not a Doper".

My dad moved us to Bend during my seventh-grade year, and I attended Pilot Butte Middle School. I wanted to play football, but I was scared to death to walk home in the dark after practice. My dad worked swing shift and couldn't pick me up, so I ended up quitting football. While attending Bend High School, I experienced fear when other kids bullied me. I was a smaller-built teenager with a loud mouth, and the other bigger kids would call me dirty names like Pip S--t. My high school years were not a good experience for me as I feared running into the bullies. One of my coaches said I needed to lift weights and learn to be quieter.

As I neared finishing high school, I wanted to become an Oregon State patrolman because I always enjoyed helping people. As I began to check out the program, my friend's dad talked to us about learning a "trade," which we could always fall back on for income. Even though we all headed in different directions, I decided to learn how to install floor coverings. At seventeen, I moved to Longview, Washington, to begin my work in floor coverings and stayed from 1977 to 1980. After Gretchen and I married, we ended up moving back to Salem, where I worked simultaneously in the floor covering business while volunteering as a youth sponsor and leader for the Calvary Temple in Salem.

Duane and Gretchen laughed when asked, "How did you meet?" Duane lovingly looks over at Gretchen and smiles, "Well, I was sixteen and camping at Prineville Reservoir on Memorial Day weekend 1975 with my close friend and his family. As I stared across the green lawn, I saw a beautiful young teenage girl with dark hair, a string bikini, and the longest legs I had ever seen. Duane laughs, saying, "I think I fell in love with her at that very moment."

She was camping with her dad and playing with her girlfriends on the lawn. I told my friend I was going to go over and talk to her, and he said, "She is only thirteen and won't give you the time of day." But I decided to go over to see her anyway. As I talked to her, she seemed very shy, and my friend was right, "she didn't give me any attention at all...she just turned and continued to talk to her friends." Gretchen laughs, "I was only thirteen and didn't care about or know about boys yet, so it was easy to ignore him." They both laughed.

Duane didn't give up. A few months later, he asked Gretchen's mom if he could have permission to take her out, and her mom boldly said, "Duane, she is only fourteen years old. You are seventeen." "No, you cannot." Duane didn't give up, "Could I just take her to Dandy's drive-up for a coke?" Gretchen's mother looked intently at him, admiring his tenacity, and said, "Okay, but have her back in one hour by 4 pm…no later!"

Since Gretchen was so young, couldn't date, and didn't show much interest in him, Duane decided to date other people in high school, but the corner of his eye was still on Gretchen. Being three years older than Gretchen, Duane graduated from high school and left for Longview, Washington, to begin his floor-covering work.

He remained friends with Gretchen's family, including her older sister, Denise, who was also his friend in high school. There were no cell phones in those days, and long-distance rates for talking on the home phone were high, so Duane asked Denise to ask her sister, Gretchen, to write him a letter. She was now fifteen, and he was surprised when he received a letter from her. They wrote back and forth, and eventually, Duane asked Gretchen's family if he could come down and take her out. Now that she had turned fifteen, they agreed she could go out with him.

Duane knew he wanted to marry her; he had loved her since she was thirteen. They continued to date on weekends when he could get away and travel down from Longview. When Gretchen was fifteen, he asked her to marry him, and she said, "Yes, but let's wait until I graduate from high school." They continued to write letters, and when Gretchen turned sixteen, they finally became engaged. Before she could marry, she needed to finish high school. Determined, she succeeded in completing her high school classes by the end of her junior year.

During this time, Duane said, "My mom discouraged me from getting married because we were unequally yoked; in other words, she was not raised in the church as I had been in my youth." Gretchen said, "What must I do to be equally yoked"? She enthusiastically repeated the sinner's prayer so they could move forward. They had waited all these years for each other, and nothing would stop them from marriage.

Gretchen was seventeen, and Duane was almost twenty when they married on August 18, 1979, at the Faith Center in Keizer, Oregon. They had a small family wedding, and following a one-night honeymoon in Vancouver, Washington, they settled in Longview, Washington. They didn't care about a big honeymoon; they didn't have much money anyway. Life was simple; they just wanted to finally start their life together.

Duane laughs as he explains, "We didn't have much money but we were happy. We eventually moved to Salem, where I continued to work in the floor covering business while volunteering as a youth sponsor and youth leader at our Assembly of God church. Gretchen worked at NW Natural Gas, and we enjoyed our simple life together."

When asked when their journey with the Lord began, Pastor Duane states, "Not long after we were married, Gretchen and I dedicated our lives in 1981 to serving Him."

At the age of twenty-one, I kept having a recurring dream that Jesus had come for His church, and I had missed the rapture. This dream freaked me out. I was afraid to sleep at night because of this recurring dream. I panicked one night and even called my mom, a devoted Christian, to see if she was still here. I was so relieved when she answered the phone.

Whew, I hadn't missed the rapture! When I had the dream again, I was painting the outside of our newly acquired home. My thoughts of missing the rapture consumed me, and I quickly sat down on the front porch steps and cried. I was so distraught. I didn't understand what was going on with these dreams. I felt a little crazy and drank a big beer to calm myself.

I had everything I ever wanted: the boat, a Corvette, a pickup, and a house, and freedom to do what I wanted; yet, I was unhappy. After continually having this dream, Gretchen and I went to the Wednesday night church service; unfortunately, they did not have an altar call that evening. Four days later, we attended Sunday service, and when they gave an invitation to turn our life over to Jesus, I walked up and knelt at the altar. While kneeling and crying out to God, I felt a nudge--it was Gretchen kneeling next to me, giving her heart to God, too. Giving our lives over to Jesus was a sweet moment for both of us.

We were finally at peace, letting go of guilt and shame. We had surrendered and yielded to Jesus. The dream of missing the rapture was gone and never reappeared.

At this time, I felt a strong pull to go into the ministry, so I started in the Berean Program, where I earned a one-year certificate in ministry. Next, I studied through Global University for two years to complete my ministerial license education, and then I attended Salem Bible College to finish my ordination studies. Each day at 3 pm, after working as a floor installer, I would go to the church and ask what I could do to help for a couple of hours. I became passionate about the ministry and people knowing Jesus, giving them hope beyond what the world offered. To this day, I still feel that same passion. Nothing is more significant than receiving and knowing the love of Jesus."

Gretchen mentions, "Four years into our marriage, we welcomed Colby, our son, into our lives. God blessed us with a son on Mother's Day, May 13, 1984. Colby was a tender-hearted, quiet child with a dry sense of humor and easy to be around. He loved playing music with his guitar and still does at his church in Texas."

Duane adds, "He was athletic in school, playing football and baseball. Even though he was quiet, he was popular, well-liked, and had close friends with whom he enjoyed hanging out. He always was a hard worker. At the age of thirteen, he worked part-time during the summer on a farm, and at the age of fifteen, he added a second job working part-time at Les Schwab. He had a goal of saving money to buy a guitar he really wanted."

Colby is married to Katherine, and they have two daughters, Taylor and Finnley. They lived just a few minutes away from us until 2022 when they decided to move to Texas. Sadly, their hearts were shattered in the summer of 2023 when they lost their daughter Taylor, at the young age of fourteen, due to a tragic accident. This unexpected tragedy shocked the entire family, and we all continue to grieve our unspeakable loss.

Taylor had a 'spark' for the great outdoors, often going for drives, camping, and boating with her family. Her smile always lit up a room and her laughter was so contagious. We miss her so much. We ask God to continually give us comfort and strength as we struggle through the grief of this unexpected loss and the hole it leaves in our hearts. (During the interview, there is a moment of silence as the tears flow and their hurting hearts grieve.)

Regaining her composure, Gretchen goes on to say, "Three years after Colby was born, we welcomed our daughter Erika on the Sunday of Labor Day weekend, September 6, 1987." As they reflect on that day, Duane and Gretchen laugh that Mother's Day and Labor Day were the chosen holidays for their children's births.

Gretchen smiles, "Erika was born with a smile on her face. She loves people, especially older people. As a young girl at church, she always drew close to the older generation. As a child, she was a beautiful singer, and to this day, she leads worship by singing at her church in Texas. She tried playing the clarinet as a child, but the sound didn't come out real smooth. We laugh that the birds changed their migration route when they heard the honking from the clarinet. Even though the clarinet was not in her future, she truly is a gifted singer." Duane adds, "Erika is very outgoing, knows herself, and knows what she wants. She is married to Christopher, and they are raising their family of four children: Avery, Braelynn, Ryker, and Kayson, in the Hill Country of Texas."

Gretchen finishes by saying, "Duane and I have always enjoyed the outdoors, camping, hunting, fly fishing, and just sitting by the campfire. As the children grew up, we traveled around Oregon camping, boating, and enjoying outdoor life, such as sitting around the campfires. The kids were always involved in youth groups during the years Duane pastored churches in Silverton and Redmond. We look forward to spending more time with our families in Texas."

♡ **Kelly & Karen Kerfoot:** *Pastor Duane, we're so grateful for your commitment to bringing us God's truth and challenging us to live our lives to honor Him. We're so thankful for how you choose to live transparently as an example before us, displaying human trials of different kinds over the years and the power of Jesus Christ alive in you! Your love, faith-filled testimony, and trust in the Lord have* *made a lasting impact on us, have changed us, and caused us to grow in our own walks with Him. We love you and will miss you more than words can say.*

Gretchen, we love you. We deeply appreciate your Godly and loving support for our Pastor as his more-helpful-than-we-could-ever-know partner. For the many ways, we see you in action week after week and for the many ways that are unknown and unseen. We're grateful beyond words for your service to our church and the countless faithful prayers you've offered on our behalf. We have the utmost confidence in your integrity and abilities in the bookkeeping office. We will forever be grateful for you both.

Praying this over you: *"May the Lord bless you and protect you; May the Lord smile on you and be gracious to you; May the Lord show you his favor and give you peace" (Numbers 6:24-26).*

With much love, Kelly and Karen Kerfoot

♡ **Helen Hunt, LaNora Vargas, and Deanna Metcalf:** *We all knew Pastor Duane when he was growing up. LaNora says, "He was my brother's little buddy. Mike and Duane were great friends and remained best friends until Mike passed away to be with Jesus. They were 10-13 years old, riding their bicycles around, doing wheelies. We lived in an older home off Irving Street in Bend, a private street where we could all play outside. We were close to town and would window shop and bike pedal to the park. Duane was a cute little boy and one of the nicest people. My older sister Darlene would make cookies, and Duane and Mike would run by grabbing cookies off the counter. My older sister Deanna and my mom, Helen, always talked about having a household full of teenagers, and they had a soft spot for Duane because he was so sweet and such a nice kid." We thank you for being such a good and loyal friend to our brother, Mike. We have always said, "When you are a friend to Duane, you are a friend for life." We wish you and Gretchen the best in your new season of life.*

Love, Helen, LaNora, Deanna, and Darlene

CHAPTER 3

Ministry Life and Leukemia Trials

As Pastor Duane and Gretchen dedicated themselves to serving the Lord in 1981, they never looked back. When asked about their ministerial history, Duane states, "I volunteered as a youth sponsor and later became the youth leader at Calvary Temple in Salem from 1981-1993. Gretchen also helped with the youth group during this time."

In 1993, Duane revealed, "I accepted the Senior Pastor position at Silverton Assembly of God in the historic town of Silverton, near Salem, Oregon, where I served until 2002.

Gretchen worked part-time in the church office, and our two children, Colby and Erika, grew up in the youth group, attending every week, plus attending summer camps. We loved living there and being part of the community, growing the church, and expanding the facilities. I was in the middle of expanding the church nursery when I received a call from the Redmond Assembly of God."

In January 2002, Duane received a call from a board member of the Redmond Assembly of God asking him if he would be interested in interviewing for the Senior Pastor position. They disclosed that his name had come up several times, while the church searched for a new pastor.

Duane replied, "I told him I was happy with my position here in Silverton." The board member repeated that your name had come up from several people. Duane gracefully declined, "No, I am not interested; I am busy working on growing the church in Silverton, and I am happy here." He was encouraged to pray and think about it for ten days. Duane mentions, "I got busy working on the big remodel at the church and forgot all about it. I didn't even pray about it because I was not interested."

After ten days, the board member called back and left a message, and I felt nudged to call him back. A wise pastor once counseled me, "Sometimes God opens His hand one finger at a time and eventually you see in His open hand what His plans are for you…are you open to at least an interview?" I thought, *"Yes, I could at least interview and see where it goes…maybe God is calling me to at least consider it!"*

Gretchen and I drove over for a pre-interview with the board, and they asked us to come back on a Sunday to preach to the congregation and have a question-and-answer session with the congregation. After praying, we agreed, set a date, and returned with our family. Colby was a senior in high school and not really excited about moving and changing schools. Erika, an eighth grader, was not keen on moving either.

I preached on that Sunday, and one man came forward and accepted the invitation to give his life to Jesus. He cried, and I held him crying, too. The moment was emotional and very moving. During the same evening, the congregation came together to ask me questions. I was surprised that there was some communication discrepancy between the board and what the congregation wanted, and I decided they were not ready for me. As the congregation proceeded to vote me in as their next senior pastor, I found myself refusing the position.

We jumped in our Suburban, paid for our motel, and headed home. As we were quietly driving through the little town of Sisters on the way back to Silverton, Colby mentioned that the man who gave himself to Christ during my sermon was worth the trip, even though I didn't accept the position. Colby, a senior in high school, saw God move and commented on it.

Two months passed, and the Redmond Assembly of God board member called me again and said, "They had corrected the communication discrepancies, and they were now ready for me. Would I consider taking the position?"

After we discussed it as a family, I resigned from Silverton Assembly of God in June 2002, stepping out in faith that if the Redmond Assembly of God congregation didn't vote me in again as Senior Pastor, God would have a different door for us to walk through. They did so with a 70% vote and the rest is history.

Twenty-two years later, I can say, "I have enjoyed pastoring at Redmond Assembly of God by loving people, caring about their lives, and being part of their spiritual growth. There are "thorns" in all jobs, but I did my best to deal with them. It is what God has asked me to do."

One of the biggest thorns Gretchen and I had to face together was in 2010 when I learned I had prostate cancer. Being told you have cancer is so devastating. After much prayer and researching all treatment options, I opted for surgery to remove the cancer. We were looking forward to that 'cancer free' proclamation after surgery, but that wasn't to be.

During the prostate surgery, the doctor removed some suspicious lymph nodes, and he was concerned there was another form of cancer present in my body. Two weeks later it was confirmed I also had an additional, unrelated form of cancer known as chronic lymphocytic leukemia. This leukemia is a type of cancer in which the bone marrow makes too many lymphocytes. Early on, there are typically no symptoms. Later, the symptoms include non-painful lymph node swelling, tiredness, fever, night sweats, or weight loss may occur for no apparent reason. The doctors assured me everything would be fine saying, "We can't cure you, but we can treat you by knocking down the disease for a while when it needs it."

The doctors watched during the first four years and tested my blood every six months. I still felt like I had a death sentence watching, waiting, and worrying, since there is no cure for leukemia. In 2014, my blood count levels climbed sky-high. I started IV chemotherapy treatments three times per week every 28 days for six months. The first IV session would be eight hours long in the Oncology Department of St. Charles Medical Center; the second day would be four hours, and the third day would be four hours. The treatments made me grossly sick and exhausted.

Gretchen mentions that this diagnosis "Rocked our world—we didn't know how long he had to live. Everything we read gave us eight years as a possibility. I tried to counterbalance Duane's worry; by being hopeful but we prepared for the end, just in case. As we look back, we did our best everywhere we went, whether to church, the doctors, or the grocery store, to show our 'light' and not dwell on the diagnosis. Duane may have days when he doesn't feel good, but God gives him the strength and courage to stand up and share God's Word."

Duane recounts, "Shortly after that treatment my Bend Oncologist retired, and it was discovered through bloodwork that I was in an unfortunate 'select group' of CLL (chronic lymphocytic leukemia) patients with high-risk, poor-prognosis markers for this type of leukemia. I was referred to a specialist in Eugene for treatment since there was nothing else they could do locally for me at that point. We traveled to Eugene, which is three hours away, for the next seven years, (often times every week for the first several years). It seemed as if there were any 'uncommon' side effects, I would get them. Gretchen called me an 'overachiever' (They both chuckled).

In 2016, I started a new clinical trial, which made me very sick. I couldn't breathe, and I kept getting infections. While we were thankful that the blood count was better, I was tired, exhausted, weak, and in a brain fog." Gretchen mentions, "He never lost his hair, and the true blessing was that he never looked sick, even though he didn't feel good. When he would preach, he would be feeling horrible, but didn't look sick, so many people didn't know he had leukemia unless he confided in them. This was a true blessing from God."

The staff at Redmond Assembly of God was truly amazing and a real blessing to us. They stepped in to take up the responsibilities as I went through treatments and recovery. Over the years, Associate Pastors Curt, Brigham, and Jeremy were here to give sermons, while Maria held down the office admin-istration. In 2016, Bryan came on board as the youth leader, followed by Pastor Belle in 2019. They all took part of the reins and did an excellent job supporting me through the long journey of ups and downs. God blessed me with such loving people.

In 2017, the doctors started me on another clinical trial for three years, where we traveled to Eugene every Thursday for the first few months (eventually we celebrated going only twice a month, then once a month, then quarterly). This treatment was a chemotherapy clinical trial in the form of pills and while they worked on the cancer, I continually still felt the side effects. Gretchen mentions, "We tried making the best of those trips, so they wouldn't feel like "just another doctor visit" by going the night before my appointments. In the morning we would head for early morning labs and after the appointments have a lunch or dinner date at the Roadhouse restaurant, visiting malls, special features, and on occasion, get pedicures. A few times we'd make it a fun trip with our travel trailer and go on side trips when Duane felt energetic enough to hike or take a grandchild along to the Springfield wave pool or take a short trek to the coast. Audible books were a huge help for the hours of driving, and we always kept our eyes on Jesus, knowing He was in control of our destiny."

In 2021, Pastor Duane states, "I started another round of chemotherapy for six months with a new drug they were able to administer here in Central Oregon. I wasn't as sick with this treatment as previously noted with my first chemotherapy. The doctors told me if the next drug did not work, I probably would only have two years to live, but you know God is good. I am still alive!"

In 2024, I live a new normal as the new drug I started taking three years ago is still working to keep my blood count down. I never feel 100% with fatigue, brain fog, and some balance issues, but I do feel better than in the past. I feel I still have some gas in my tank to live life. The Lord brought in the new leukemia drug at the right time and I am able to be treated locally at this point. We are grateful and appreciate what the Lord has done.

Gretchen mentions, "When you go through this as a couple, it makes you appreciate each other more. You sort out what is important and thank God for every moment together. Duane, facing his own mortality and losing ten members of the congregation to unexpected deaths in 2018, turned out to be an overwhelming year. He traveled to Eugene every Thursday for a year making an appointment to see a Christian counselor to help monitor the traumatic stress. We thank each doctor, nurse, and medical staff member who helped us. They, indeed, are a gift to us." Duane finishes by saying, "Yes, 2018 was a tough year. While having leukemia treatments and losing so many members of our congregation, it was truly overwhelming. I remembered that God is in control of our lives, and all we can do is trust Him and 'love' each other until we go home to be with the Lord."

Yet, through the many years of treating leukemia and facing the stress of losing ten members of our congregation in one year, Gretchen and I were not prepared for the biggest challenge and shock that changed our lives forever.

♡ ***Hank and Sharon Weldin****: We walked into Redmond Assembly of God in June 2003. And, wow, so much has happened since that day. Everyone was very friendly. I was so self-conscious due to my throat surgery, and I had difficulty talking. The compassion was such a blessing to both of us. On our second visit, the Pastor remembered our names. You have an incredible gift. We're so blessed to have met you both and that you've become our great friends.*

We've had some great times together. You two have become family, and we so appreciate you loving us, our children, and our grandchildren. We've laughed and cried together in good times and sad times. You are so special to both of us.

Thank you for everything you did to start and support Celebrate Recovery, which allowed us to represent our church. I know you both will have a ball in retirement. It's fun to watch your excitement about the Pippitt Farm. We're only a call away, don't be strangers. Love, Hank and Sharon

♡ ***Loren and Vicky Roff****: God truly blessed Loren and I when he sent us to Redmond Assembly of God. Pastor Duane and Gretchen are the example of integrity and leadership. You have shown each of us, as Christians, how we should live our lives each day. Love and blessings to you both, Loren and Vicky*

CHAPTER 4

Unbelievable Grief

THE WORDS ARE STILL HARD to say! We lost our sweet fourteen-year-old granddaughter, Taylor, on June 30, 2023. There is nothing in life that prepared us to hear such shocking news. Gretchen reflects, "It started when we received a quick text from our daughter-in-law in Texas saying, 'Urgent: Pray Immediately. Taylor has been in an accident and has been taken to the hospital by ambulance. I don't know anything yet.'"

We waited, and later in the day, we learned that due to the seriousness of her injuries, she was being flown by helicopter to the nearest children's hospital in Houston, Texas, a few hours away. Our hearts sank.

We immediately purchased airline tickets to Houston, but felt frustrated that we couldn't fly out until the following morning. We arrived in Houston around 6 pm on June 30, 2023, only to learn that due to her traumatic brain injuries, she has only a few hours to live. The shock to our hearts is surreal, almost like you can't grasp what is happening. In the ICU, with all the family surrounding her, we pray for a miracle that she could be healed, but as the evening progresses, we prepare to say our emotional goodbyes.

The grief and intense pain is beyond words as we struggle with the disbelief of "what has just happened"? Everyone is devastated and numb as we cry endless tears, and faces hang down with sad, unbelievable grief. Gretchen and I feel incredibly helpless as we watch our son and his wife, and Taylor's younger sister, struggle to grasp the unsurmountable trauma of losing Taylor.

Pastor Duane, with grief in his voice, looks down and says, "There are no adequate words to describe such a heartbreaking loss, and the shock leaves our hearts completely traumatized. How does one make sense of knowing she was out enjoying her friends one afternoon and the next evening she is gone? Our family is left trying to cope as we painfully cry while our hearts break into a million pieces. She is so young, and her whole life is ahead of her. I cry, "Why couldn't it have been me—I am older and sick with leukemia? I wished I could take her place." None of this makes sense.

As a pastor for forty-one years, I have had a close relationship with Jesus, and I know God's promises, but I can't help but cry out, "Why, God? Why? I believe in Jesus with all of my heart, and as believers, we understand God's purposes are only for good, yet in the middle of our heartache, I cry out, "Why, God? Why did this young child have to die?" Nothing makes sense as our emotions spill over into intense pain, suffering, and shattering grief.

With tears spilling down her face, Gretchen softly states, "I don't know how to put it into words. As horribly painful as it is for us as grandparents, I just can't imagine being a parent, losing a child. Watching our kids lose their daughter adds layers of heartbreak. Taylor gave me the biggest gift when she was born by making me a Grandma. They lived in Redmond then, and I spent quality time with her, seeing her often. When she was six months old, I pulled her highchair into the kitchen and while propped up with baby blankets I started "teaching her" how to make chocolate chip cookies. For years, until they moved to Texas we made all kinds of cookies together. It was one of our special bonding moments. It has taken me nine months, since she died, to even bake cookies again."

Duane shares, as they reflect on the memories, "She has such a contagious laugh, one of those gut laughs deep from within." I love to tease the girls by saying, "Hey, there are my two pretty girls," and they would giggle and laugh. Some of our best memories are of camping and boating. Taylor loved the outdoors and loved to swim, boat, and surf on a wakeboard. She was like a water dog, always loving the water. We always enjoyed sitting around the campfire sharing the day."

Gretchen tearfully laughs at the memory of "Screaming in the carwash as the brushes washed the car. Taylor had so much fun screaming with Grandma in the carwash. I also have wonderful memories of camping, playing the piano together, and making cinnamon rolls and homemade noodles together. There are so many memories, but these I hold close to my heart."

Gretchen repeats one of her favorite scriptures in Psalms, a gentle reminder that God had recorded all of our days before we were even born. This gives us peace that Taylor lived a full life in the eyes of God.

You made all the delicate inner parts of my body
And knit me together in my mother's womb.
Thank you for making me so wonderfully complex!
Your workmanship is marvelous --- how well I know it.
You watched me as I was being formed in utter seclusion,
as I was woven together in the dark of the womb.
You saw me before I was born.
Every day of my life was recorded in your book.
Every moment was laid out,
before a single day had passed.
How precious are your thoughts about me, O God.
They cannot be numbered!
I can't even count them;
they outnumber the grains of sand!
And when I wake up,
you are still with me!

— (Psalms 139:13-18)

As Duane and Gretchen reach for more Kleenex, Duane tearfully says, "Losing Taylor struck us to the core and I couldn't help but ask God Why? Why Taylor? Yet, we kept on praying and praising Him. We cry heavy tears, but we looked to Jesus for comfort; we hurt deep inside, yet we kept on worshipping the Lord we know and love through the pain."

Pastor Duane states, "You may be surprised that even seasoned believers like pastors and ministers, who have been preaching for years and know about Jesus' promises, may still ask, "Why, God?" We are human, and extreme loss hits us just like everyone else. We know God walks beside us, yet in the middle of shocking grief, our minds are in a thick fog, unable to find the comfort we need."

Nonbelievers may ask, "If God is such a loving and powerful God, why would He allow an innocent child to die?" Unfortunately, nonbelievers may suffer additional emotional and mental pain as they grieve and mourn, unable to find the peace believers may experience as they grieve. Believers know that God did not "cause" the death to happen, but He does allow events to occur for reasons we won't know until we get to heaven. Believers understand God's purposes are only for good, yet in the middle of our heartache, we may still cry out, "Why, God? Why?" We hurt, and we don't understand.

We know Jesus loves us as He walks alongside us, offering us comfort and strength to keep on going each day. As a family, we recognize Jesus's love through the love of those around us. His love may come through the love of family, friends, neighbors, sympathy cards, emails, flowers, kind words, caring people, therapy, or grief counseling. Jesus' love knows no boundaries.

The Sunday after this tragic accident, Jeremy Hocker, our associate pastor, spoke to the congregation, saying, "For me today, it is a sad day. It is a sad day for our pastor's family. It is a sad day for all of us here in the congregation. Do you ever feel like God doesn't answer your desperate prayers? We thank You, God, for helping us with our unbelief. We believe, God, that You are alive and active, yet we wonder if You hear our desperate cries. Do You care? We doubt ourselves as we struggle. We may even feel angry with God for the injustice in the world, especially when the good ones are taken. We don't understand why children's lives are cut short.

God wants us to speak to Him when we are going through difficult times. He can handle our anger, frustrations, and bitterness. He is a strong God who is good, and He can manage those hard, searching questions, especially if we stay in the spirit of Habakkuk 2:1, which reads, "I will climb up to my watchtower and stand at my guard post. There, I will wait to see what the Lord says and how he will answer my complaint."

Pastor Jeremy went on to say, "Every human emotion is the stuff of prayer. We deal with things like joy, hatred, anger, depression, anxiety, and frustration. God is good, and He modeled for us that we should speak to Him whatever we are going through—speak to Him about our disappointments, struggles, questions, and concerns.

When God hears our cries, He may not respond as we expect Him to because God knows what is best for us. God is bigger than us and knows the plans for everyone's lives. He sometimes allows us to groan and cry for reasons we don't know. His silence does not equate to His absence. He is always beside us."

We see in the New Testament Paul encourages people to bring every concern to God in prayer and enjoy the resulting peace of God, described in Philippians 4:6–7 (NKJV)

"Be anxious for nothing, but in everything by prayer and supplication, with thanksgiving, let your requests be made known to God; and the peace of God, which surpasses all understanding, will guard your hearts and minds through Christ Jesus."

Many will ask, "How long? How much longer shall we suffer?" We read in the Scriptures where David prayed to God:

O Lord, how long will you forget me? Forever?
How long will you look the other way?

— Psalm 13:1

Have compassion on me, Lord, for I am weak.
Heal me, Lord, for my bones are in agony.
I am sick at heart.
How long, O Lord, until you restore me?

— Psalm 6:2–3

Pastor Duane says, "After Taylor's memorial, Gretchen and I returned home to Oregon three weeks later. I wasn't ready to give any sermons, but the other pastors encouraged me to move forward, even in my grief, so the congregation would know we were alright. My response was, "But I am not alright." After some thought, I decided to share our journey of pain and grief even though I wasn't sure I was up to it."

On the first Sunday back to church, Pastor Duane quietly shared with an emotional, crackling voice, "Lord, be with us in the middle of this crisis. We need help understanding. This is not easy! We worship You. We cry out to You. Father, we look up to You. We praise You and lift up Your name. Oh, Lord, we hurt! We give You praise and glory. This is a territory we have not walked through before. Lord, losing a grandchild so young and innocent tears us apart. We always believe You know best, yet we have no words. The words don't come to adequately describe how we feel, how we hurt, and how we grieve.

We have cried so many tears, and through the pain and suffering, this is one of the first times in forty-one years of ministry when I have asked, 'Why, God?' We know Your words, Lord; we know Your promises; and through our lifetime of learning about You, we know and stand on Your faithfulness as we grieve our loss.

Lord, I don't have any answers and don't understand, but I continue to trust in You. I continue to praise and sing to You. We will not know the 'why' on this side of heaven, but there is one thing I do know this morning, and I believe this with my whole heart as I stand here today."

God is faithful,
God is true,
The Word is true, and
He will be with us until the end.

Pastor Duane sadly reflected, "In the ICU, when Taylor left to meet Jesus, I leaned down and whispered in her ear, 'I will see you in a few minutes.'" As believers, we know the separation is only temporary, and we will soon be together again. I know, in my heart, that she is in heaven, that all is well, and that I should rejoice. But the frail, human side of me cries because she is gone, and we will deeply miss her. I hurt so much, my strength fails, and my heart aches for my family.

The shock is difficult to describe. It feels like the time when I fell off a horse straight onto my back. As I hit the ground, all the air in my lungs was knocked out. I gasped and struggled to breathe, but no air came; my brain was foggy, and then slowly, I felt the air starting to fill back into my lungs. That is how it has been for the last few weeks."

During one of the following Sundays, Pastor Duane once again quietly spoke, "Being a seasoned pastor, this is the first time in my entire life I have asked the question, 'Why, God?' In my fourteen years of battling leukemia, I have never asked, 'Why, God?' I just accepted that I had the disease and asked God to lead me through the treatments. But losing our granddaughter at such a young age and knowing we won't get to watch her grow up is so heartbreaking."

We keep reminding ourselves we will get to see her again soon, and when that day comes, when we are united, we will be happy, the answers will be revealed, and it will be good. Until that time, how do we get through this grief and suffering? We keep worshiping, we keep singing, and we keep on trusting God, over and over. We keep on trusting Him every minute of the day."

In Devotional Daily, there is an inspiration that reads, "Sometimes you may say 'God is good,' with tears running down your cheeks. He is good, and He will see you through and He never wastes your sorrows. He didn't waste the sorrows on His Son on the Cross, and He won't waste your sorrows. By His magnificent power, He will transform them into that which is good for the Kingdom and glory to His name."[1]

The pastor finished his talk with this: "Help us, Lord! We are struggling. My prayer is that everyone will come to know You, Lord. You know it was a true blessing that my teenage granddaughter dedicated herself to the Lord to love, praise, and follow Him again during a recent church camp. After her memorial service, I see young teenagers holding hands in a circle and praying and giving their lives to You, Lord. Is this what it is all about? One person's life ends to save the lives of others? Does that child inspire others to turn to You, Lord?"

Gretchen adds with tears, "Taylor and her younger sister were scheduled to fly to Oregon and stay with us for two weeks on July 15, 2023, the day of her memorial. It was heartbreaking when my cell phone went off with a reminder that I was supposed to pick them up at the airport on that date. It was like a stab to my heart that she is gone.

The Scripture says, *"And we know that all things work together for good to those who love God, to those who are called according to His purpose"* (Romans 8:28 NKJV).

We also know, in Isaiah 55:9: *"For just as the heavens are higher than the earth, so my ways are higher than your ways and my thoughts higher than your thoughts."*

The strength and power of our pastor's words inspire all of us. We grieve with him through his grief and feel the love of Jesus speaking through him. The pastor's message is that no matter what we are going through and no matter how hard it gets, the Lord is with us to give us the strength and comfort we need each minute of the day. The Lord said we would have trials in life—and some trials are harder than others.

As the pastor explains--our hearts go out to them, "Even in the midst of our grief, it is okay to ask why—yet we pray; we hurt—yet we pray; we cry— yet we pray. We pray knowing Jesus is with us. We pray knowing Jesus' ways are right, and His ways are good. We draw close to Him as we continue to trust and lean on Him. We turn to family and friends as we express our sorrow and encourage each other to stay close to Jesus."

Our pastor loves singing one of the old hymns that represent our desire to trust in Jesus. It is one of his favorite songs:

> Tis so sweet to trust in Jesus
> Just to take Him at His Word
> Just to rest upon His promise
> Just to know, "Thus saith the Lord."

Jesus, Jesus, how I trust Him
How I've proved Him o'er and o'er
Jesus, Jesus, precious Jesus
Oh, for grace to trust Him more

Pastor Duane states, "The Lord never leaves us if we follow from our hearts and not from our heads. The heart is the seat of our emotions, and through the tough trials, He is there for us. My heart knows I trust Jesus, yet my head goes to 'Why, God?' We need to pray and say the name of Jesus over and over and over to stay in His heart."

Pastor ends his sermon with what we read in Scripture: "*Trust in the Lord with all your heart, and lean not on your own understanding*" (Proverbs 3:5 NKJV).

As families grieve with broken hearts, the Lord knows something we don't know or completely understand. If one family member dies, the grief and love of twenty to forty other family members is an extended-release of love for that person and each other. This release of love through grief extends to each other as we cry, comfort, and give words of encouragement. We may continue for years to share our grief and love for our child, extending our love to neighbors, friends, church, and work.

This is Jesus' love. His commandment is to love one another as He has loved us. Believers' souls, when they die, will immediately be in heaven with Christ Jesus. This may result in more family and friends turning to Jesus for salvation. The Lord knows who will come to know Him and be with Him for eternity. One person's unfortunate death may result in hundreds to thousands of others being saved, Dr. David Jeremiah, the pastor of Shadow Mountain Church in California, writes in his bestselling book, *God Has Not Forgotten You*: "

Perhaps the only thing worse than thinking whether God has forgotten us is the idea that God has forgotten those in our family. Watching our loved ones suffer or try to find their way through trouble may be one of the most difficult things to endure. We want so desperately to help! We want to make things right, and we sometimes have difficulty understanding why God doesn't step in to do just that."[2]

On the following Sunday, still raw from grieving, Pastor Duane shares, "As a dad, it has been hard watching my adult son and family hurt as they grieve. I have always been able to offer advice or fix things that needed to be done. It is what we do as a dad". Pastor looks down and softly says, "When my grieving son became quiet, he asked me, 'What do I do, Dad?' I was at a loss for words, and it hurt. All I could say was, 'Honey, I just don't know."

Dr. David Jeremiah writes, "God offers us three ways to respond in such moments. You can replace fear with faith, sorrow with God's Word, and your heartache with trust in God."[3] We may not know the answer right now, yet we have a bit of peace knowing that someday, when we reach heaven ourselves, the answer will be clear, and it will be good. All we can do right now is trust God. Sadly, while we are in the grieving process, we need extra help to get us through the sadness, loss, and pain.

Dr. Earl McQuay, a minister who lost a son in a tragic car accident, wrote a small book entitled *Beyond Eagles: A Father's Grief and Hope.* In this book, he offered a special note to parents and families who have endured the death of a child. He listed five realities that provided immense comfort to his heart and to his wife's:[4]

The first reality is ***Scripture.*** The Word of God serves as firm ground as the hurricane of tragedy sweeps over our souls. Scripture, God's promises, truths about heaven, and comfort in Scripture all drew us closer to the Lord.

The second reality is ***prayer.*** With prayer, you can cry out to the Lord, knowing He sympathizes with you. He answers by giving you the support of others, cards, flowers, or just an encouraging word. In prayer, we can rest in God's arms, find comfort, and trust Him to turn our heartaches into memories and eventually praise.

The third reality is ***friends.*** At the time of your greatest need, the members of the body of Christ come to offer comfort. Their prayers encourage us and help us to heal.

The fourth is ***memories.*** We gave thanks for the years we had with our loved ones, remembering the smiles, laughter, adventures, and good times together.

The fifth is ***hope.*** For the believer, death is not final—only a pause until we can be together again.

In summary, there are not enough comforting words to reduce a parent or grandparent's pain, yet the God we serve and love can give us emotional comfort while we are here on earth. God is everlasting, and He has prepared a place for each of His believers. He has your child in His protection, giving them a safe place of love and joy until you see them again. What a joyful day that will be. We can comfort one another with His Word.

> *Weeping may endure for a night,*
> *But joy comes in the morning.*

— Psalms 30:5 (NKJV)

♡ ***Donna Hay and Jerry Kelly*** *want to thank you both for your example of a strong Christ-centered marriage and for your humble grace fighting the battle of leukemia treatments. When difficult losses came up unexpectedly in life, you were not afraid to ask God why. Your transparency of sharing real life with us helps us too, to live closer to God. We appreciate everything you and Gretchen have brought to the ministry and we will miss you both dearly. We love you! Jerry and Donna*

♡ **Floyd and Debi Dobkins:** *Where do we start writing about such a special couple? We had the fortune of attending grade school with Pastor Duane, so it was* *a huge blessing when we voted him in as our new Pastor twenty-two years ago. We have many fond memories of time spent with Pastor Duane and Gretchen. They have taught us so much, leading by example, and we are very grateful for their servant hearts. When Pastor Duane preaches, he has a way of illustrating what he is teaching that helps bring the Word of God to life.*

They taught us how to genuinely care for people and helped us through some of the most challenging times of our lives. We will never forget the morning that we received the news of our seventeen-year-old granddaughter's passing. Our son Tim called Pastor Duane that morning since they found out before we did, and he and Gretchen showed up at our home within minutes after our daughter called us to let us know. They were there for us and helped us with all the planning for her Celebration of Life, and they continued to check in with us and support us through our grieving for months. We can never thank them enough for their love and support, and we will love them both always and forever! Floyd & Debi Dobkins

CHAPTER 5

Retirement Plans

WE HAVE EXPERIENCED MANY TRIALS throughout our lives, just like every one of you. God gave us the discussion and plan to retire, and we both wholeheartedly look forward to what lies ahead. Following the Lord is the beauty of waiting for His loving nudges and moving forward in peace to accomplish His plans for us.

When asked, "How do you want to leave here after being lead pastor for twenty-two years at Redmond Assembly of God?" Pastor Duane replied, "As I prepare to retire, I am pleased that I am leaving it better than when I came on board. We are financially sound, paying down the mortgage debt to a respectable level. We purchased additional property next to the church, re-did the parking lot, renovated the commercial kitchen, installed the welcoming porches at the entrances to the sanctuary building during an entire exterior remodel, and so many more projects. We continued to build on this church's legacy for years, supporting missionaries worldwide, and baptizing people, marrying couples, and honoring many end-of-life funerals. We consistently communicate about Jesus' love and how we can serve and praise Him. We couldn't have done any of it without the body of Christ. Our members are genuine Christians who love Jesus.

As I look back, Gretchen states, "One of my favorite moments in ministry was planning and leading mission trips to Kenya and Nicaragua, which left me with many memories. I went with Convoy of Hope and several other members of our church. I appreciate the bonds I made with others as we worked side-by-side. When you visit third-world countries, you learn to appreciate where we live and what we have. We met children who walked barefoot for one mile in dusty Kenya to get food and water and never complained."

What do I hope to accomplish before Gretchen and I retire? First, I want to relieve some pressure on our church board by performing some of the day-to-day duties, while they search for a new lead pastor. Secondly, I want to finish strong. Redmond Assembly of God is in good shape, and I want the next lead pastor to step in knowing they don't have to worry about undone maintenance and finances. They can love the people and share the sweet message of Jesus.

When asked, "What legacy do you want to leave behind?" Duane responded, "I told Gretchen that on my grave marker, I want it to say, "I told you I was sick." (Just kidding, they both laugh.) I hope people know that I loved them, cared about them, was faithful to my calling, and was honest with what God asked me to do. I hope they remember that I loved my wife, children, grandchildren, parents, and the rest of my extended family, which is all of you."

After forty-one years of ministry, they are asked, "What do you plan to do in retirement?" Pastor Duane smiles, "I am not sure where the Lord will lead me, but I am working on my 1965 Chevy El Camino to put in a bigger motor. My eighty-seven-year-old dad is a great mechanic, and we plan to work on it together. My dad lives close to the church, and I look forward to spending more time with him. Gretchen and I bought some acreage in Terrebonne a few years back, where we built a shop and brought in a new manufactured home. I plan to raise a few cows, haul hay, help Gretchen with a garden, and be a mini-farmer. Can you see me hanging out in denim overalls with my dogs (my counselors)?"

Duane says, "We bought our acreage in July 2020 and it had an old 1971 single-wide mobile home on the property that was extremely run down and neglected for years. The previous owner left it in "as is" condition, including her dentures on the table. We planned and ordered our new manufactured home, only to discover that it would take another fourteen months to build. We had ordered our new home during the height of COVID with employee shortages and hard-to-get building supplies. It was quite a shock to learn we had to wait so long. Since it was getting too cold to stay in our travel trailer and the pipes were freezing, we decided to fix up the old single-wide to live in while we waited for the new one. It had two bedrooms, one bath, and an additional extra room in bad shape."

Gretchen comments, "The kitchen was gross with greasy, dirty cabinets. I wore a mask and gloves and took a sledgehammer to some kitchen cabinets that were extra greasy. The refrigerator was a mess, and the freezer was left unplugged for three months with food left in it. You can just imagine the smell! We took turns gagging as we cleaned it out. Skunks were under the trailer and it had broken sewer lines when we bought it. Can you just imagine the smell and the cleanup?

We cleaned, repainted, and installed a few new floors to make it livable. As we tore out four layers of dirty carpet, Duane noticed the linoleum under the carpet was the same pattern he grew up with as a young boy. We thought that was funny. We ate off paper plates and used plastic utensils because we didn't have a dishwasher. The furnace was the original from 1971, so I felt like I was living in a fire trap as we reconnected all the heat registers. All-in-all, we saved money and made it work, while we waited for our new home. The Lord has a way of keeping us humble during trying times."

Duane mentions, "After cleaning up the place, we did okay, even inviting people over for Bible studies and dinners. In August of 2022, we moved into our new home, built a pole barn, and put in a fence. We are much more comfortable." (They both laugh as they reflect back on that time in their lives.)

Duane continues, "Many people don't know this about me, but my favorite animals are cows. We usually raise four Red Angus cows to eat and share with others. They are so peaceful and spend their days moseying around the pasture eating grass. The cows lie down and regurgitate their stomach contents by chewing their cud until one day they become 'ground beef.' Gretchen loves to name each of the cows like Juicy Lucy, Rosy the Ribeye, Salisbury Sally, and Ginger Beef.

I love growing and hauling hay, moving the irrigation equipment, playing with the dogs, and sitting around the backyard campfire with Gretchen, and often friends and neighbors. My family and Gretchen bless me daily and mean the world to me. All of this gives me great peace. Oh yes, I forgot, I love watching college football in the fall. Go OSU Beavers and Texas Christian University!"

Gretchen smiles and says, "In retirement, I will work for Synergy from home, doing some financial work associated with the Oregon Ministry Network of churches. We used to camp all the time, but now, with our little farm, we don't even have to leave home. We spent years camping, hunting, and fishing with the kids in Oregon with our travel trailer. Our favorite hideaway is Delintment Lake near Burns, Oregon, which we have always found secluded and serene. (Don't tell anyone because it is still quiet and secluded.) It is a great place to go and refresh our spirits.

Nowadays, we enjoy staying home and sitting around our outdoor campfire with our black and yellow labs, Mac and Gus. (Duane calls them his counselors.) I inherited three barn cats with the property and made it my daily mission to pet them at feeding time—it took over a year, but two of them occasionally let me pet them now. They don't let Duane come near them (as Gretchen says with a smile). I still love to sew and plan to create more sewing projects. Our biggest passion is our family, and we plan to spend more time with Duane's dad, Del, and our sisters here in Oregon. We will have more time to visit our children's families in Texas. We are grateful for those special moments with each of them."

♡ **Claudine and Chuck Day:** *Thank you, Pastor Duane and "First Lady" Gretchen for your devoted dedication to us for so many years. You have touched our souls with God's Word for many years, being the best Shepherd(s), leading and guiding us through thick and thin. Our true forever friends! You have earned a blessed retirement. May you have peace, joy, divine health in Jesus' name during your retirement. Rope, ride, fish and drive to your heart's content. We love you two! Claudine and Chuck*

♡ **Shane and Deanna Van Winkle**: *My wife, Deanna, and I first met Pastor Duane and Gretchen ten years ago at Redmond Assembly of God. The first thing I noticed is that they manifested a calm spirit as a couple. My wife mentioned that the ladies were all so friendly and made her feel welcome, so we decided to make this our church home.*

We noticed right away that as husband and wife, Duane and Gretchen both had strong spiritual and leadership abilities. Together they made a strong and caring spiritual couple who exhibited Godly qualities.

I actually met Gretchen, a few years before, at the city office where I obtained job permits for my excavating business. She talked about her husband being the pastor at Redmond Assembly of God and invited my family to come and visit.

I was involved in 1978-79, as a temporary laborer on the framing crew that built the church building here on Antler, plus volunteered on the building program with many others.

I noticed that Duane was a great shepherd and mentor working with the younger men who were striving to be in the ministry. He always encouraged others to preach or learn from him. He didn't need the glory; he truly wanted to mentor and see everyone grow in their work. He constantly poured out his life into building and equipping others for the ministry.

I once told Duane, I wished I could 'transport him back in time' and have him be my mentor when I was a younger man. I was serious with that funny comment.

Man to man, Duane led by example when it came to morning devotions and prayer time with God. It convicted me about my own walk with the Lord and challenged me to do the same. I know he had health issues and a lot on his shoulders, but he kept on going. I knew if he could do it, I could do the same. I admired his commitment and his qualities as a Christian man.

I love Duane and Gretchen's industrial nature. They bought some acreage with an older home on the property. They were planning to put in a new home, while living in the older home. As an excavator, this was a challenge making sure the utilities worked for both places. Gretchen shocked me with her working knowledge of construction. She could engineer and draw out how to install gate valves, back-flow devices, electrical conduits, and sewer and water lines. She understood how everything had to work to function. Duane would always say, "Ask Gretchen how that works...she is the construction boss here. I loved it!"

They worked together building fences and they both loved to run the equipment. It was fun to watch Duane drive the 10-wheeler dump truck and Gretchen drive the loader tractor. They both had big smiles on their faces as they worked in the dirt, loading and hauling it around their property. They both work well as a team and can both do just about anything.

Gretchen is also a carpenter....what?? Both Duane and Gretchen played a major part in building their garage and shop. They are great craftsman and I was amazed on much work they did on their structures. The inspectors were impressed how well they did too. Gretchen did say it sure helped having fresh maple bars on the day of the inspections. We laughed!

Duane loved excavating and he would say, "Wow, if I wasn't a full-time pastor, I would love to do what you are doing". We laughed at "maybe we could have been business partners."

I have to say, Pastor Duane and Gretchen did a fine loving job leading RAG, but they are physically hard-working people outside of church. There is not one lazy bone, in spite of Duane's health issues, in his body. I marvel at their ability and stamina.

Deanna and I wish Pastor Duane and Gretchen well on the next phase of their journey. They are loved and respected by so many people. May God richly bless them both. Shane and Deanna Van Winkle

CHAPTER 6

Thank You to Our Staff

PASTOR DUANE SERIOUSLY STATES, "As we look forward to retirement in August of 2024, we think of the wonderful people who served on the Redmond Assembly of God staff. As a pastor, you never really know who the Lord will bring into your circle of influence. The Lord has called all of us as followers of Christ to make disciples (Matthew 28:19-20 paraphrase). Very early in my first years as a senior pastor, I felt the Lord speak to my heart about rising up young men and women, who felt the Lord's call, to full-time ministry. I felt so strong about this because, although I had great educational training, I never really had a genuine mentor who put their arm around me, and walked and showed me what it meant to a pastor.

Completing ministerial training and obtaining opportunities are two completely different things. I have always felt that the Lord gives some pastors the ability to have insight into other's individual qualities they can't see in themselves. For example, a new pastor may have the gift of teaching, but they may not see themselves as having the gift of teaching. They need to be encouraged, developed, and given opportunities to use their gift of teaching. A pastor, who is a true mentor, must be willing to share the spotlight to encourage others to use their gifts. Many pastors find this hard to do.

A true mentor sees their staff as co-workers; all willing to serve God. We all are serving God in the same capacity, just using different job descriptions. So as a pastor leading a church family, I feel strongly that you have to offer those called alongside you opportunities to work in the ministry. As a pastor, the Lord hasn't asked me to turn others into who I am, but to help them develop their skills and spiritual gifts into the best possible version of themselves. With the Lord's help, they will be the best they can be. We must become cheerleaders, encouragers, builders, and lifters of those called alongside us. We become coaches who share the wins and suffer in the defeats alongside them.

In Bible College, one of my professors said, "Before God allows you to fulfill His calling on your life; He will use you to help someone else fulfill their calling". This part of the mentoring process is sitting in second or possibly, third chair, even though you might feel ready to take the reins. The Lord sees if you have a humble heart, a teachable spirit, can handle correction, or if you are becoming prideful, needing all the attention and the limelight shining on you alone.

Over the years God has truly blessed me with some wonderful people. I have been able to share the ministry with people. I might call my inner circle. Those people God has allowed me to invest in, mentor, and encourage them in the ministry. One is now a missionary, three are lead pastors in their own churches, and the three people I am currently working with, as I near retirement, are true gifts to me.

In the twenty-two years I have served at Redmond Assembly of God, Associate Pastor **Jeremy Hocker** has been by my side for twenty-one of them. He has been a faithful co-worker, a spiritual son, and a true pleasure to work with through the years. He is always willing to go above and beyond his daily tasks and has become a very close friend to me. After all these years together, he still walks into my office two or three times a day and asks, "Do you need anything?" He is and has been a faithful companion, and I don't have enough words to express how much I love and appreciate him.

Pastor **Bryan Brannon**, our Family Life Ministry pastor, has been a part of our team since 2016. Pastor Bryan is also a dear friend and co-worker. He has a tender shepherd's heart and loves the ministry the Lord has called him to. He loves the Lord's church and desires to see the church family healthy and moving forward in their relationships with God and each other. He also has been a faithful companion and true son in the Lord. Once again, I don't have enough words to express my love and appreciation for him.

Pastor **Belle Gould** is our youth pastor. When she joined our team as an intern in 2019, she had just graduated from college. She was here to help with our communications systems. Yet shortly after her arrival, it was evident God had a call on her life for pastoral ministry. She received her ministerial license and moved into the youth position when Pastor Bryan took over the family ministries role. She is excellent with the youth and doing a wonderful job. Around the team, she is fondly referred to as Joseph since the other team members think she is my favorite. There might be a little truth there, but I will keep that to myself. And, once again, I don't have enough words to express my love and appreciation for her.

When I affectionately think of these three people, the word that comes to mind is ***servant***. All three have faithful servant's hearts, willing to take on any task required or asked of them without complaint, and they do it with excellence.

We have learned and grown together in ministry, and it has been my greatest privilege to share this season of ministry with them. They all know I love them and have very high expectations for them for the future. I truly believe they will exceed any accomplishments we have done together and do greater things for the Lord than they can imagine. The three of them have made me better, and I trust it has been the same for them. I will continue to be their greatest cheerleader, only now from a distance.

Our office staff has also been a gift and a personal blessing. My wife **Gretchen** has been our administrator and bookkeeper for fifteen years, and **Maria Corbin,** our church secretary, has been here longer than anyone else on the team. The two of them have worked tirelessly going above and beyond what is asked of them or anything on their job description. The ministry areas these two ladies have helped with over the years are endless. They are always willing, actively participating, leading, organizing, making things happen, making everything run smoothly and efficiently. These are qualities both of these ladies possess. They have done it all with a smile and kindness in their hearts. It has been a privilege to work together with them.

Through the years, I have served with many wonderful board members, ministry leaders, other staff members, and volunteers who love this church family. They have been diligent in prayer, planning, and helping lead our family of believers. They have walked beside and counseled those with deep wounds and hurts and we have witnessed together the power of God to heal, restore and redeem people's lives. Again, the possibilities of those blessed with opportunities to use their spiritual gifts, become a blessing to each one they encounter and it's all done for the glory of God the Father.

We have so many wonderful memories and friendships established through the years. I will miss serving this family in this capacity. Yet, Gretchen and I remain humbled that the Lord has allowed us this opportunity to walk with precious people, who will continue to be our lifelong friends and with the daily reminder of what an honor it has been to be called *"pastor"*.

> *The master said, 'Well done, my good and faithful servant.*
> *You have been faithful in handling this small amount,*
> *so now I will give you many more responsibilities.*
> *Let's celebrate together!'*

> — (Matthew 25:23)

♡ **Nancy Blankenship:** *Pastor Duane and Gretchen, your ministry is a labor of love, defining you and all you have poured into the body of Christ at Redmond Assembly of God and beyond. Together, you forged healing, love, integrity, compassion, acceptance, growth, joy and fun. Thank you for following the call to RAG and sharing your lives. You have impacted the lives of so many for eternity, walking alongside and shining a light on the path.*

It seems a lifetime ago that I was scared and uncertain to serve on the board. Still, it's been a blessing and opportunity beyond what words can express. I'm grateful to have listened to God's small voice and said yes.

I appreciate your friendship and sharing life for oh, so many years. I can't imagine these past five years without your love and support. You are both a gift that keeps on giving and giving.

Praying this next chapter of your life is filled with all the experiences, joy, laughter, and things your hopes and dreams have anticipated, like adventures at the gas pump, crazy cow stories, and oodles of time together and with your family. Live and enjoy every day to the fullest. Nancy Blankenship

CHAPTER 7
Saying Good-Bye

As an author, (Susan Free) I would like to sincerely thank the fellow pastors, staff, board members, volunteers, and people of the Redmond Assembly of God congregation for their sincere messages blessing Pastor Duane and Gretchen. These messages throughout the book are heartfelt and demonstrate the love and respect each of you have for them as they retire. My sincere apologizes to anyone I missed, as contact information was not available for everyone.

"Dear friends, let us continue to love one another,
for love comes from God.
Anyone who loves is a child of God and knows God"

— (1 John 4:7).

 *Associate Pastor Jeremy Hocker*

Pastor Duane, you are a person of love and compassion, guiding me on a journey of deep and unconditional love for others. Your leadership has taught me the transformative power of empathy and kindness. Your unwavering dedication to fostering a culture of love has inspired me to extend grace and understanding to those around me. Your gentle guidance and unwavering support have empowered me to embrace love as a guiding principle in my interactions, fostering deeper connections and enriching the lives of those I encounter.

One of the most admirable qualities of Pastor Duane is his complete lack of jealousy towards others. Instead of harboring envy, he radiates genuine joy and celebrates the successes of his staff and congregation. His humility sets a powerful example, encouraging all of us to root for the achievements of others and champion their endeavors with unwavering support, lifting and empowering those around us.

Pastor Duane's commitment to promoting and defending his staff is a testament to his integrity and loyalty. He recognizes each individual's unique talents and contributions, tirelessly advocating for their growth and well-being. His open-door policy extends not only to his staff but also to the youth in the church, creating a nurturing environment where every voice is heard. Through his availability and accessibility, Pastor Duane models what it means to be a servant leader, embodying the teachings of Christ in his actions and words. Amidst his dedication to nurturing relationships and fostering community, he remains steadfast in preaching our hope in Christ, reminding us of the boundless grace and love that anchor our faith journey.

I am thankful for all that Pastor Duane has taught me in the twenty-one years that I have worked with him. He is a friend and a grandpa figure to my children, as well as my pastor and my boss. Thank you, Pastor Duane, for believing in us and reminding me often to "be nice."

Erin and I wish you and Gretchen a retirement of watching the flames of the campfire, playing with your counselors, and enjoying your free time. Associate Pastor Jeremy Hocker

♡ *Pastor Bryan Brannon, Family Life Ministries*

Bryan Brannon, Pastor of Family Life Ministries says gratefully, "These are the words that come to mind when I think of my pastor and leader, Duane Pippitt:"

Humble, Supportive, Champion of Others, and Empathetic

I came to the Redmond Assembly of God's staff in October 2016, accepting the youth pastor position. My wife, Jamie, and two children, moved here from Washington and quickly fell in love with our new community and new church. I soon recognized that my new pastor and boss was the same person in staff meetings as he was behind the pulpit. He led and spoke with humility. He never demanded that we follow his orders. He would suggest what we should do, invite our feedback, and then make a decision. In almost every case, his decisions were made from a collective perspective, all of our voices together.

Pastor Duane has always supported and encouraged us on the team. He has continually backed it up by speaking so highly of us, and frequently, from the pulpit. Something I wasn't used to seeing. He champions us regularly. Encourages us often, and shares his pulpit without hesitation. He sees our strengths, weaknesses and supports us as we wrestle to balance them within ourselves and our ministries.

I know there were times I would share a "bright" idea I had, and he would give me a smirk, shake his head, and then proceed to say, "Go ahead!" as if to say, "You're a little crazy, but I'll let you try it." He let me be me and discover who I was called to be in ministry. The one thing I have learned most from him has been how he loves and empathizes with his congregation.

I've watched this man carry the weight and burdens of our church, including the loss of loved ones, his cancer diagnosis, and the storms of life that cloud our vision. Not only has he led himself through these very struggles, but he has also walked hand-in-hand with hundreds of families as they navigate their trials.

I have learned to see people with greater compassion, slowing down to see them where they are. And I've learned that loving people is a constant discipline, a muscle to develop, an action to perform when we sometimes crave that same love from others. In Proverbs 11:25 it states, "...*those who refresh others will themselves be refreshed.*"

Pastor Duane and Gretchen, thank you isn't enough. You've loved, supported, and championed me as I continued to discover my calling and journey. I know I was the cause of a few headaches. Yet you let me be me. I am who I am today, much in part because of you. I am forever indebted to you, and I hope to continue your legacy in my own ministries as I model who I am after you. Step into your retirement with joy and great anticipation. God's not done with you! Again, I say, God's not done with you!

 ### *Youth Pastor Belle Gould*

Wow, how do you put into words two people who have impacted your life in such a monumental way? Pastor Duane and Gretchen have played huge roles in my life over the last six years. They have been so much more than my pastors and mentors. They are my family.

If you look up the qualities of a family and the qualities of a mentor, the definitions both have so much in common. Duane and Gretchen embody these qualities. A family is a group of people united by some tie (marriage, blood, adoption) who interact with one another in their respective social positions. The "ideal" family can be defined as a unit providing support and stability to each member. Each person feels valued, respected, appreciated, and understood. Families foster room for growth, learning, and emotional well-being. Members of the family share the responsibilities, keep promises and are very loyal to each other. It is effortless for family members to trust one another.

A mentor is a person who facilitates the personal and professional growth of the individual they are assisting or coaching. Mentors do this by providing guidance and support and transferring knowledge from the experienced mentor to the mentee. A great mentor has excellent listening skills, is honest, and can give constructive feedback to help another grow. At first glance, the two seem different, but when you really get deeper into the roles each plays, you see that a mentor can become family very quickly and that a family can mentor you quite easily. Both listen, support, direct, and value the people involved. Duane and Gretchen have taught me much about ministry, loving Jesus, and growing as a person.

As my mentors and my chosen family, Duane and Gretchen, have taught me not only about ministry and being a pastor but also so much about myself.

They are two of the biggest cheerleaders in my life, and because of their love and support, I believe in my calling to ministry. I moved to Oregon in 2019 as a twenty-one-year-old college graduate, and I had no idea what a life in ministry would entail. Pastor Duane not only shared his years of experience and stories with me but always ensured I had a seat at the table.

I remember when I first came on the team there was a meeting for all the ministers in Central Oregon. I was just a church intern then and didn't fully realize what the Lord had for me, but Pastor Duane did. I was fully prepared to be left at home to take care of my church intern duties, but Pastor Duane brought me along because I belonged in the room with the pastors. This was a life-changing moment for me. My leader made the space for me to belong even before I knew I was supposed to belong. This moment inspired my desire to pursue my credentials and officially gain the title of "pastor." Pastor Duane's support was not a one-time thing; he has always given me a chance to preach on Sunday mornings, speak my mind in meetings, and be in the room with other ministers.

I have never questioned where I stand with Duane and Gretchen; I know I am one of their favorites, and I am pretty sure everyone else knows it, too. Around the office, I gained the nickname "Joseph," which is Jacob's favorite son. My "brothers" Maria, Bryan, and Jeremy recognize that I have a special place in Pastor Duane and Gretchen's heart. As much as I would like to believe that I genuinely am their "favorite," I have also witnessed that they have an amazing gift for making everyone feel valued and special. If you spend enough time around them, you will feel like their favorite, too!

There is always room at the table when you are with Duane and Gretchen; they have so much love, kindness, and forgiveness to share with people. God's love oozes out of them. They are always consistent in who they are. I have seen them on good and bad days, and in whatever life throws at them, Duane and Gretchen lean into the love and faithfulness of God. I am so thankful that God gave me the opportunity to be part of this team and be led by these two amazing people. Knowing Duane and Gretchen has changed my life forever.

Jared and I will always have fond memories of our 2023 marriage when our whole "family" supported us and shared in our happiness. With Love, Pastor Belle Gould

♡ **Maria Corbin**: When Pastor Duane and Gretchen arrived at the Redmond Assembly of God, Pastor Duane made positive changes through his dedication to prayer, patience, and perseverance. His commitment to uniting the congregation with wise decisions and the careful selection of pastors brought healing and created an atmosphere of genuinely loving each other. Pastor Duane and Gretchen both live what they preach. They love God with all their hearts and have a passion for people that is evident in everything they do.

I have enjoyed watching Pastor Duane mentor the younger pastors and seeing the pride in his eyes when they take the next steps in their ministerial journey. Investing in people's lives is what they do. I don't even know if we could quantify the lives they have affected.

Both Pastor Duane and Gretchen have been profound teachers in my life. I often find myself reflecting on their wisdom. Gretchen's reminder that 'your lack of planning does not constitute an emergency on my end' and Duane's advice on tossing (into the round basket) complaints without signatures, has become some guiding principles for me.

Over the course of twenty-plus years, we have weathered many changes together. Through the good and the challenging times, I have always found solace in the unwavering support of Pastor Duane and Gretchen. They are not just pastors or coworkers but family to me, always ready to lend a hand in any aspect of my life.

They both have a great sense of humor, which makes working with them fun. In the early years, I was always running into work from taking my kids to school, and when I arrived, there was always something that needed to be done right away. So, I would often leave my purse on my desk chair. Later, I would look for it but could not find it. Eventually, I would find it in the **freezer**. Duane always claimed he was looking out for me and keeping my purse safe.

Gretchen is also a prankster. In addition to having a great sense of humor, she has pulled off some pretty funny pranks. I'm just going to leave it at that... laughing!

I know that God still has great things in store for them. I love them both very much. Maria Corbin

♡ **Sharon Mergel**: I love many things about Pastor Duane, not only for his excellent teaching and advice when I needed it, but also for his great sense of humor. Many, many times, he would tell a story that would make fun of himself; making us laugh and liking him for it. Happy New Beginnings! Love in Jesus Christ.

I can't fit my praises for Gretchen into one paragraph, but I ask everyone to read Proverbs 31:10-31. She fits this perfectly. She has served us well. Love You Both, Sharon Mergel

A Wife of Noble Character
Who can find a virtuous and capable wife?
She is more precious than rubies.
Her husband can trust her,
and she will greatly enrich his life.
She brings him good, not harm,
all the days of her life.

She finds wool and flax
and busily spins it.
She is like a merchant's ship,
bringing her food from afar.
She gets up before dawn to prepare breakfast for her household
and plan the day's work for her servant girls.

She goes to inspect a field and buys it;
with her earnings she plants a vineyard;

She is energetic and strong,
a hard worker.
She makes sure her dealings are profitable;
her lamp burns late into the night.

Her hands are busy spinning thread,
her fingers twisting fiber.
She extends a helping hand to the poor
and opens her arms to the needy.
She has no fear of winter for her household,
for everyone has warm clothes.

She makes her own bedspreads.
She dresses in fine linen and purple gowns.
Her husband is well known at the city gates,
where he sits with the other civic leaders.
She makes belted linen garments
and sashes to sell to the merchants.

She is clothed with strength and dignity,
and she laughs without fear of the future.
When she speaks, her words are wise,
and she gives instructions with kindness.
She carefully watches everything in her household
and suffers nothing from laziness.

Her children stand and bless her.
Her husband praises her:
"There are many virtuous and capable women in the world,
but you surpass them all!"

Charm is deceptive, and beauty does not last;
but a woman who fears the LORD will be greatly praised.

Reward her for all she has done.
Let her deeds publicly declare her praise.

— Proverbs 31:10-31
Blessings, Gretchen

♡ **Carl and Wanda Graffenberger** shared a humorous story about asking Pastor Duane and Gretchen to go to Kauai, Hawaii, in June 2004. The Graffenbergers had a timeshare in Kauai and offered to share it with the Pippitts, and they said, "Yes, we would love to go." We had a great time sightseeing, eating, and swimming at the beaches, and even the Pastor went snorkeling. He wouldn't run and play in the ocean surf with us, though.

One day, we were looking for a beach that wasn't so crowded. We spotted a beautiful beach with a vast field of weeds and bushes between the beach and us. Three of us said, "No, we will pass on this beach" because it looks too far to walk to the beach. Plus, it had a large metal cattle guard gate that was locked. We would have to climb over it to get to the beach. Gretchen said, "Trust me, just trust me, we can walk to that beach." She said it over and over, convincing us that we should try it. Well, doesn't everyone trust the Pastor's wife?

I was the first one over the gate, and something big had previously fallen hard on the gate and bent the top rung. Gretchen accused me of being so overweight that I bent it. We all laughed and laughed. (Yes, we are still friends today.)

We all managed to climb over the metal gate. We headed through the brush, avoiding cow pies, sticker bushes that scratched our legs and swiping away insects. As you can guess, that was the last time we considered the "Trust me" statement. Plus, one could assume we were trespassing by climbing over a locked gate.

However, the Lord protected us through all the fun and laughter; otherwise, we could still be in jail on a beautiful tropical island with an awesome prison ministry on our resume.

Thank you, Pastor Duane and Gretchen, for such a fun trip to Hawaii—a trip we will never forget. We wish you nothing but the best for your retirement years. Carl and Wanda Graffenberger

♡ **Cindy & Rod Shaver; Jan Lueck and Joe Noel**: Where do we start? Duane and Gretchen, through our eyes, you are God's gifted Shepherds of Men. You have set the tone of benevolence at Redmond Assembly for twenty-two years. We want to share with you both how much we have appreciated your honesty, transparency, and humility. Duane, your sermons have inspired and shown your great faith. The sermons have also combined human fragility with a delightful sense of humor. Although there are many instances that we could speak about events that have made your and Gretchen's ministry so successful, we would rather speak to the kindness and love you both have shown to all your flock during your tenure at Redmond Assembly of God. Best wishes for your retirement. God Bless You! Love your brothers and sisters in Christ.

♡ **Brooke Highsmith**: Pastor, I could never have known what you would come to mean to me when you took the helm of this church all those years ago. You immediately drew me in with your warmth, humor, and self-deprecation. Week by week, I listened as you laid yourself bare from the pulpit, and I thought, here is a man, humble before God, who loves the Lord with all his heart. I found wisdom and life lessons in your sermons. I felt the Spirit's touch through your prayers.

And, unlike other pastors I had known, you became my friend. I've loved laughing with you, sharing meals, and swapping stories. Thank you for trusting me when I didn't trust myself to be able to take on the responsibilities of serving you and the church as a member of the Board. You made me grow in ways I couldn't have imagined. I am blessed.

Gretchen, there is no more important job for a pastor's wife than to be a support and helpmeet to her husband. Your beautiful example of loving him made all of us love you. How wise you are! Your strength, compassion, and practicality demonstrate your clear understanding of your worth in God's eyes. This is not to say your talent at taking on the recording and reporting of the financial well-being of our church has gone unappreciated. I stand amazed.

Knowing and loving you both has enriched my life. So, this cannot be a goodbye. Instead, it is simply "See you later, my friends." Until we meet again on the other side of all these changes, may God walk beside you and pour His blessings all over your lives. With Love, Brooke Highsmith

♥ **Mike and Deborah Cook:** We met Gretchen and Duane Pippitt when we started attending Celebrate Recovery in 2017. At that time, we were on staff at another church and were always impressed by their love for the Lord. In 2021, we were asked to become Ministry Leaders for Celebrate Recovery and became members of Redmond Assembly. Pastor Duane and Gretchen understood the sacrifice to change churches and were so gracious with that transition. One time, they took us out to dinner, and it was wonderful to have them all to ourselves. Then they added a trip to the frozen yogurt store, and we talked long into the night. They have meant so much to us, and we consider them close friends now. Congratulations on your retirement! Mike and Deborah

♥ **Ray Murphy:** My time working here at Redmond Assembly of God under Pastor Duane has been such a blessing in my life. I have always been able to go to Pastor Duane if I needed to talk about anything, and he would always welcome me. I always say. I've been blessed beyond measure to have a boss as caring and loving as Pastor Duane. The atmosphere of the office was always fun and relaxed. Working with Gretchen was great as well. Gretchen was always so helpful with whatever I needed. She was always forward-thinking to make the office ran as smoothly as possible. They both made working at Redmond Assembly of God more fun and productive. We are a team. They always made sure to make you feel welcome, and your opinion mattered.

♥ **Steve and Bev Rosen**: We have greatly appreciated the ministry of Pastor Duane and Gretchen Pippitt. When we began to get acquainted with them, we discovered that our good friends were in their church in Silverton, so we had that in common. When Pastor Duane learned that Bev was raised as a Quaker, he asked if we knew of a pastor friend who also pastored a church in Silverton. We knew of him, but not on a personal basis.

In May 2003, Bev was asked to interview for the church bookkeeping job with Pastor Duane and a board member and was hired. It was such a privilege for her to work with them at the church until October 2009. In 2005, our son Curt Rosen and his wife and family were asked to be the Associate Pastors and were on staff until 2011. We so appreciated Pastor Duane speaking into Curt's life and showing him the many aspects of being a well-rounded Pastor.

Thank you, Pastor Duane and Gretchen, for being who you are and for your love for each and every member of our congregation. Thank you for being transparent with us in all areas of your lives. We will continue to pray daily for you and your family. Love Steve and Bev

"Then Christ will make his home in your hearts as you trust in Him.
Your roots will grow down into God's love and keep you strong.
And may you have the power to understand, as all God's people should,
how wide, how long, how high, and how deep His love is.
May you experience the love of Christ,
through it is too great to understand fully.
Then you will be made complete,
with all the fullness of life and power that comes from God"

— (Ephesians 3:17-20).

Sermons

A Firm Foundation
Commitment to God
Pursuing God
Understanding Contentment
The Golden Rule
Facing Impossible Situations
Cultivating Thankfulness
Easter – Life Changing
Understanding Communion
Mother's Day – Empowering with Encouragement
Father's Day Message
The Importance of Missions
Christmas Story of Salvation
A Heavenly Place

CHAPTER 8
A Firm Foundation

PASTOR DUANE ASKS THE CONGREGATION, "What is the most important part of any structure you decide to build? If you are building a house, barn, sky-scraper, bridge, an apartment or hospital building, what is the first thing to consider? Your answer would most likely be 'the foundation.'"

You see--it doesn't matter how beautiful, architecturally modern, or glamorous a structure is because it will eventually fall without a proper, strong foundation.

One of the greatest and best-known examples in the world today is the Leaning Tower of Pisa in Italy. It was initially called the Tower of Pisa, not the Leaning Tower of Pisa. The tower was renamed five years after construction when it began to lean due to poor soil.

In the Bible, Jesus warns us of such things in our own lives. Jesus certainly understands that for any Christian to lead and have the kind of life He intended us to have, you must first lay the foundation in your life.

Having a proper foundation built on Jesus' words is so important. A foundation that won't allow you to lean back towards the life that Christ has saved you from, a foundation that won't allow you to lean back towards the world, but a firm foundation that will keep you walking perfectly upright and standing straight for Jesus.

In Matthew 7:24-29 we read, *"Anyone who listens to my teaching and follows it is wise, like a person who builds a house on solid rock. Though the rain comes in torrents and, the floodwaters rise and the winds beat against that house, it won't collapse because it is built on bedrock. But anyone who hears my teaching and doesn't obey it is foolish, like a person who builds a house on sand. When the rains and floods come, and the winds beat against that house, it will collapse with a mighty crash. When Jesus had finished saying these things, the crowds were amazed at his teaching, for he taught with real authority—quite unlike their teachers of religious law."*

Here, Jesus tells us the proper, Godly way to lay the foundation for our lives. Why did Jesus say this? He said it because he knew storms were coming our way. There are always storms in our lives; we need to expect them and prepare for them. We have all had storms, such as health issues, financial concerns, relationship problems and worries about our children, disharmony at work, and even difficult times in the church.

Jesus wants us to have a firm foundation to stand on and to be prepared for storms as the winds blow and the sands shift. Jesus asked (his disciples), *"Do you finally believe? But the time is coming—indeed, it's here now—when you will be scattered, each going his own way, leaving me alone. Yet I am not alone because the Father is with me. I have told you all this so you may have peace in me. Here on earth, you will have many trials and sorrows. But take heart, because I have overcome the world"* (John 16:31-33).

This is God's blueprint for us to follow. If we follow it, we will find success. If we decline it, we will discover inevitable failure, but it's your choice. It is my choice to follow God the best I can.

In these two verses of John 16:31-33, Jesus says that anyone who hears His words and does what He says to do is a wise person. Did you notice that Jesus doesn't say that if you sit through a forty minute sermon without falling asleep, you are a wise person? He doesn't say that reading your Bible fifteen minutes a day or praying three times a day makes you wise.

Although those are all beautiful things and things we should be doing, Jesus says, "First, hear my Words." All wisdom is found in walking in obedience to His Words.

When I was young and growing up in the church, my mom was strict with me about going to movies, dances, and playing cards. One day, I asked her if I could go to the movie "The Computer Wore Tennis Shoes" (which seemed harmless to me), and she said, "What does your conscience say?" Even though the movie seemed harmless, my mom had given me the foundation to always ask myself, 'What does your conscience say?' (I did go to the movie.) She would also say, "Flee the very appearance of evil". Today's society is making evil look good and good look evil, so unless we are rooted in the foundation of Jesus' Words, we can be easily be fooled.

Isaiah 5:20 (NKJV) states, *"Woe to those who call evil good, and good evil; Who put darkness for light, and light for darkness; Who put bitter for sweet, and sweet for bitter."*

In Luke 6:47-49 it says, *I will show you what it's like when someone comes to me, listens to my teaching, and then follows it. It is like a person building a house who digs deep and lays the foundation on solid rock. When the floodwaters rise and break against that house, it stands firm because it is well built. But anyone who hears and doesn't obey is like a person who builds a house right on the ground, without a foundation. When the floods sweep down against that house, it will collapse into a heap of ruins.*

Jesus says a proper foundation for your life comes through hearing His Words, applying them to your life, and living them out daily. These two things are handcuffed together. Doing one without the other should never happen.

Hearing and applying is the second step in building a firm foundation.

Why come to church and sit through sermon after sermon? Why read your Bible at home day after day or attend bible studies if you're not going to apply what you've heard and learned?

Without hearing God's Word preached and reading your Bible regularly, it will certainly not lead to living a life pleasing to God. The two work together.

Jesus says in Romans 10:17, *"So then faith comes by hearing and hearing by the word of God* (NKJV). In other words, a wise person does both of these things. Hearing and applying the Word of God will be an everlasting foundation for your life. If you choose to listen, read, and study God's Word and build on your life with the words you have learned, you will be able to stand firm when the storms of life hit you square in the face.

You will stand when you receive bad news. You will stand when you get laid off from work, and you will stand when the stock market crashes. You will stand when that phone call comes from the doctor saying you have cancer, and you will stand when things take an unexpected turn. Why? Because there is always a storm coming!

Because you have learned that Christ is enough. He will take care of you, he will provide for you, He will comfort you, He will give you his peace, and He will meet your every need.

You will stand because your life is built upon the rock, and that rock will hold you firm. If your foundation is cemented to the rock, you will not waver.

Now it's apparent here who that rock is. The Bible states in 1 Corinthians 10:3-4, *"All of them ate the same spiritual food, and all of them drank the same spiritual water. For they drank from the spiritual rock that traveled with them, and that rock was **Christ.**"*

We also learn in 1 Corinthians 3:11, *"For no other foundation can anyone lay than that which is laid, which is Jesus Christ"* (NKJV).

In Ephesians 2:19-22, the apostle Paul wrote this to the church members in Ephesus, the same as God is telling us here today:

"So now you Gentiles are no longer strangers and foreigners. You are citizens, along with all of God's holy people. You are members of God's family. Together, we are his house, built on the foundation of the apostles and the prophets. And the cornerstone is Christ Jesus himself. We are carefully joined in him, becoming a holy temple for the Lord. Through him you Gentiles are also being made part of this dwelling where God lives by his Spirit."

Paul clearly reaffirms the teaching of Jesus that we previously read in Matthew 7:24-29. Paul says that if you have accepted Christ as your personal savior, you are no longer a stranger or foreigner to God; you are now a citizen with the saints of the household of God.

Your foundation was built by the apostles and the prophets, but Jesus Christ is the chief cornerstone, the main stone, and the most important stone in that foundation.

It's no coincidence that Jesus is referred to as the cornerstone. Each time the Jewish people built their temple, they used a primary cornerstone. The first stone laid was the most perfect in the foundation. All other stones followed the perfectly laid cornerstone, which was perfectly plumbed, perfectly square, and perfect in every aspect.

What would happen if the actual cornerstone was imperfect and the other stones were laid against and on top of it? They would begin to lean. They would follow the shape of the cornerstone, which is the same as your own foundation in life.

In your life, Jesus Christ has to be the cornerstone of your foundation to build your life on the rock of Jesus. If your life is built on a leaning foundation or shifting sand, your whole life will eventually lean the wrong way.

Some of you remember the old hymn, "On Christ the Solid Rock I Stand, all other Ground is Sinking Sand, all other Ground is Sinking Sand". How true that is.

It's true, not because of my own experiences, it's not true because of your experiences; it is true because Jesus says it's true in Matthew 7:24-25.

Your life, and my life to be practical and fulfilled, must be built on the Rock of Jesus Christ. You will be able to stand through every storm in Him. **Ask yourself:** Is my knowledge of Jesus and His Word increasing or decreasing from what it used to be? Am I really applying what I know about Jesus and His teachings in my life? Do you hear, apply, and know His words?

A life built on Jesus will produce a person filled with faith, which is serving Him, and fired up about Him, and what He has done and is doing in them.

It's a person who doesn't waver in their beliefs.

It's a person who doesn't compromise the Truth.

It's a person who puts Jesus first in their life.

It's a person who realizes that without Jesus, their life is without purpose.

Jesus clearly states in Matthew 7:26-27, "*But anyone who hears my teaching and doesn't obey it is foolish, like a person who builds a house on sand. When the rains and floods come and winds beat against that house, it will collapse with a mighty crash*". In other words, your world will eventually crumble if your life is not built on the Rock of Jesus Christ. Many need to note this important fact in this verse.

Jesus doesn't say that it's impossible to build on the sand. You can build on the sand, and something built on the sand, whether it's your life, a business, your home, or even a church, may appear to be flourishing, but Jesus' word is apparent here that eventually, it will crumble.

Today, many Christians look around and see other people flourishing. We see the unsaved or people who claim to be Christians, but don't show the fruit of being a Christian doing well in business or as church members. They might look like they are doing well, and we tend to think, "What's happening here?" We shouldn't worry about other people, their business or other churches. We need to pay attention to our own walk with the Lord.

It is best if you focus on your life. Is your life built upon the perfect rock, the chief cornerstone of Jesus Christ?

Know His Word, study it, and, most importantly, apply it to your life.

James 1:22-25 tells us, *"But don't just listen to God's Word. You must do what it says. Otherwise, you are only fooling yourselves. For if you listen to the word and don't follow it, it is like glancing at your face in a mirror. You see yourself, walk away, and forget what you look like. But if you look carefully into the perfect law that sets you free, and if you do what it says and don't forget what you heard, then God will bless you for doing it."*

Parents, I want to encourage you to first show your children that Jesus is the foundation in your life as you lay a solid foundation for your children's lives. Are you telling them that He must be what they build their lives upon because everything else will fail?

The Tower of Pisa quickly became the Leaning Tower of Pisa. The original builders in 1177 did not expect the tower to start leaning, but five years later, it just happened to lean because they needed to lay a proper foundation. It took five years before it leaned one inch. That improper foundation held that building straight for five years, but through the storms, rain, and wind, the building began to lean gradually as the ground started to sink. Through the years, it went on to lean 15 feet, and they kept shoring it up, hoping it would not someday fall. The tower could not stand straight on its own because its' foundation began to sink on one side.

Jesus may not be your foundation right now. You may be living a life without Jesus, thinking you're making out just fine. But I promise you, if your feet are not deeply rooted in Jesus' Word and if you are not applying Him to your life daily, eventually, that sand under your feet will start to sink slowly, and you will begin to lean.

You'll eventually lean back into the sins that Jesus saved you from. You'll eventually begin to slip and lean away from Jesus and His will in your life.

Maybe that lean has already begun to happen for you, or maybe the sand beneath your feet has already begun to sink. Sinking sand can look like drinking more alcohol, smoking marijuana because it is legal, looking at pornography on the internet, spending money unwisely, or looking lustfully at the woman/man you work with. These are just a few of the things that start people down the path of sinking sand.

As a pastor, I sometimes counsel with young couples. This particular couple was in their thirties and they came to me with their frustrations of being in debt. They had purchased a big home with a high mortgage, bought two new cars, and ran up credit card debt where monthly payments were high. The woman said, "Why is God doing this to me? I am mad at God for putting us in this position."

The Bible says, "People ruin their lives by their own foolishness and then they are angry at the Lord" (Proverbs 19:3). Sometimes we can recognize people by their own fruit and how then contribute to making life more difficult.

The best we can do, in all cases, is earnestly repent, ask the Lord for His forgiveness, and re-commit to Him. Make Jesus the foundation for your life from this day forward, and apply what you know to your life. Life will look different and change for the good.

Christianity is not about religion or rituals; it's about Christ. That's it. So don't let the devil destroy your foundation. Keep him from mixing clay in with your iron.

As I close, I want you to remember this: In our passage today, we are told we will walk on either rock or sand, with the rock representing Jesus and the sand representing the world.

What will exhaust you quicker, walking on a concrete sidewalk or walking on the beach?

Walking on sand might be more fun for a short time, but it is exhausting. Walking in this world without Jesus might be fun for a short time, but it will begin to exhaust you, leaving you tired and empty.

If you have leaned away from Jesus, come back to Him today.

If you have made Jesus the rock of your life and His Word the foundation of your life, keep going, keep moving forward.

I love the movie 'Top Gun Maverick'. I think I have watched it over forty times. Tom Cruise, being a Navy Top Gun pilot for over thirty years says in one of the scenes, "It's not WHAT I am, it is WHO I am". Being a pastor and knowing Jesus, is not WHAT I am, but it is WHO I am. We are all children of God, it is WHO we are. Jesus is our Rock.

Remember these three things that Jesus needs you to do:

Hear My Words

Hear and apply what you learn

Know the Words

When Jesus is your foundation, the world may despise you, But your LORD and SAVIOR will LOVE .you.

What means more to you? Is Jesus worth putting Him first in your life, not just on Sunday, but every minute Monday through Saturday?

Remember the old hymn: On Christ the Solid Rock I Stand, all other Ground is Sinking Sand, All other Ground is Sinking Sand.

> *"Anyone who listens to my teaching and follows it is wise,*
> *like a person who builds a house on solid rock"*
>
> — (Matthew 7:24).

♡ **Sunny Rae:** *Rich Mullins, the late Christian musician, once said he "wasn't saved by learning the nuts and bolts of Christianity, but by being with Christians* *who were the nuts and bolts". Duane and Gretchen, you are the nuts and bolts in my book and I wish you all things good and holy.*

♡ **Angus and Sandra McDonald:** *We have been eternally blessed, Pastor Duane and Gretchen, to have been part of your flock, under your watchful care, beneficiaries of your spiritual teaching, feeding in green pastures that you have led us to and most importantly, enveloped by your love for us. In our spiritual and Christian journey of many years, we can honestly and thankfully say that you are excellent and faithful shepherds. You have fulfilled the pastoral calling defined in 1 Peter 5: 2-4. We have never felt as loved, nurtured, or protected in our Christian walk. Indeed, your journey and ours are not ending, just changing, and we are confident that it is God's will and promise that we take what we have learned and move forward, spreading the same love of Christ that we have been blessed to have known under your leadership. May God bless and keep you in your next chapter of this life. We will forever be family. Angus and Sandra*

CHAPTER 9

Commitment To God

WHAT DOES IT MEAN TO commit to God? How many of you know that a partial commitment is no commitment at all? Committing ourselves to Jesus is a big commitment, but one, we will never regret. He wants all of us to spend eternity with Him.

Jesus always said that the person who follows Him must be all in. In Luke 9:23, Jesus said to the crowd, *"If any of you wants to be my follower, you must give up your own way, take up your cross daily, and follow me."* Jesus never made an exception. If he ever did, it would have been when a rich young man came to follow Jesus.

Scripture tells us, *"Teacher, what good deed must I do to have eternal life?" Jesus replied, "Why ask me about what is good?" "There is only One who is good. But to answer your question, keep the commandments to receive eternal life." The man asked Jesus, "Which ones?" Jesus replied, "You must not murder. You must not commit adultery. You must not steal. You must not testify falsely. Honor your father and mother. Love your neighbor as yourself"* (Matthew 19:16-19).

The man was puzzled and said in Matthew 19:20-22, *"I've obeyed all these commandments. What else must I do?" Jesus told him, "If you want to be perfect, go and sell all your possessions and give the money to the poor, and you will have treasure in heaven. Then come, follow me. But when the young man heard this, he went away sad, for he had many possessions."*

Remember, Jesus isn't so interested in what you have as long as what *you have doesn't have you.* Outwardly, the man had everything that would make a great follower of Jesus. Yet, inwardly, he was holding back. Jesus recognized that the man was only able to make a partial commitment. Jesus does not want and will not accept a partial commitment. He didn't then; He doesn't now.

You see, God wants all your heart and a close relationship with you. We need to die to ourselves and our wants and follow Jesus. Listen closely to His voice and follow what He wants you to do for Him. Lord, it is your breath that we breathe; it is your breath that we praise. We praise and love you in your precious name.

Several years ago, I picked up my six-year-old granddaughter from school, and as we traveled home, I asked what she had learned during the school day. Like most kids, she slowly let her mind spin through the day and said, "Nothing." I told her that when I was her age and in first grade, I learned "nothing," too. She looked up at me and smiled slightly, unsure whether to take me seriously or not.

Then I decided to try another approach and asked her, "What was your favorite class today?" She thought briefly and happily said, "PE" (physical education). She laughed as she said, "We sang and danced the Hokey Pokey. Do you want to sing it with me?" I chuckled and started singing as we drove home:

You put your right foot in, you put your right foot out, you put your right foot in, and you shake it all about. You do the hokey pokey, and you turn yourself around. That's what it's all about.[1]

You put your left foot in, you put your left foot out, you put your left foot in, and you shake it all about. You do the hokey pokey, and you turn yourself around. That's what it's all about.

You put your right arm in...
You put your left arm in...
You put your head in...
You put your knees in...
You put your shoulders in...

You put your elbows in…
You put your bottom in…
You put your quiet voice in…
You put your loud voice in…
You put your tummy in…
You put your nose in…
You put your 'whole self' in…

Folks, this playful children's song is what it's all about. This song reminds me of the apostle Paul, who wrote, *"And so, dear brothers and sisters, I plead with you to give your bodies to God because of all he has done for you. Let them be a living and holy sacrifice—the kind he will find acceptable. This is truly the way to worship him"*(Romans 12:1). "To give your bodies" is Paul's way of saying, "Put your whole self in."

Jesus wants our "whole self," not just an arm or a leg, an elbow or a nose or a loud voice. He wants us to be totally committed to following Him, praising and loving Him, turning to Him for everything, and trusting His ways.

If I was honest, I don't think most people come into a worship service prepared to give their whole selves to God. The reason is that we bring sins that need to be confessed, questions that need answers, and problems that need solutions. We bring our burdens, anxieties, frustrations, depression, brokenness, and all kinds of distractions.

Yet, we have not fully worshiped until we give ourselves entirely to God. Worship is the total commitment of our total person for our whole lives. Real worship is not merely offering elaborate prayers to God, singing great praise, or listening to a sermon. Real worship happens when we confess and repent of our sin, turn from that sin, and then offer ourselves wholeheartedly to God.

The question remains: Why don't we give ourselves wholeheartedly when we encounter the presence of God? Why don't we fall at His feet, giving Him our all? If we realized who God is, the creator of heaven and earth, the giver of life, the one who named all the stars and set the moon and sun in place, we would have absolute reverence for Him. He loved us so much that He sent his only Son to this earth to die a cruel death on the cross, so we have the choice to live with Him forever in eternity.

If we believed this with our whole being, wouldn't our 'whole self' want to live for Him and follow Him the rest of our days on earth?

If we continue to lead a life of a sinful nature, we eventually lose it. For example, suppose a person is a chronic drinker, uses illegal drugs, continues an adulterous affair, or steals and lies. In that case, this individual will eventually lose out on life. They could lose their marriage, lose their relationship with their children, lose their job, or lose friends. You end up losing your 'whole self.' When you follow Jesus, you give up your old ways and learn to trust in Jesus. We call this "dying to the self." He shows us how we are to go, helps us get there, and saves us from destroying our lives by giving us a more content and peaceful life. We can never be perfect humans, but we can surrender our lives to Jesus for Him to mold and shape us.

Most of us are a work in progress. Worship is the total commitment of oneself to the Lord. We have all sinned. We are not perfect, and, as your pastor, I am not perfect. I live like you do. I pay bills, do things that make my wife happy, and buy ice cream for my grandkids, but I could be better and do better. My wife blesses me because she says she is happy. My grandkids bless me when they giggle and laugh with ice cream all over their face. But I also have times when I worry about a bill, or I say something unkind to my wife, or moments when my grandkids make too much noise. I am a flawed human, but I have committed myself to following Jesus while I am here on earth.

Worship is a lifestyle I lead every day. Worship is not just a song, a Sunday sermon, an offering, or fellowship during worship service. We don't leave it all here after church on Sundays. We take it with us everywhere we go. We take it home and treat our family well. We take it to work and treat our co-workers kindly. We take it to the grocery store and treat everyone with respect. We get in the car and decide not to yell at bad drivers. Everywhere we go and everyone we see, we worship God by treating everyone and everything with love and kindness. Isn't that what Jesus would do?

It is easy for people to try to control aspects of their lives, thinking God doesn't have time for them. It is easy for people to believe God wouldn't love us if He knew how we lived. It is easy to think we are not worthy or enough for God's almighty love. Yet, He loves us all with unconditional love. Turning our whole self over to Jesus offers us an opportunity to let go and trust Jesus with 100% of our lives.

So why do we offer ourselves as a living sacrifice?

1) WE OFFER OURSELVES TO GOD BECAUSE OF HIS MERCY

Apostle Paul presents God's mercies as his strongest argument for giving ourselves to God. *"I urge you,"* Paul said, *"by the mercies of God...to give your bodies"*(Roman 12:1). When we recognize what God has done for us through His Son Jesus Christ, the only response is to give ourselves entirely to Him.

We are all sinners, and that sin has deathly consequences. Roman 6:23 tells us, *"For the wages of sin is death, but the free gift of God is eternal life through Christ Jesus our Lord."*

But, while we were still sinners, Christ died for us. He took our place, taking on the punishment of our sins so that there is no condemnation for us. We avoid eternal separation from God and the fire of hell—and live in the eternal presence of God for eternity. Taking on this punishment is His act of grace and mercy. It is the ultimate gift that we must never forget.

Can I say that we are in trouble if reflecting on God's mercies does not move us? Where would we be without God's love and forgiveness? Where would we be without God's presence in our lives? What kind of hope would we have without Him?

Think for a moment about your situation. Consider your family, your friends, your job, and your church. Do we deserve these things based on our merit alone? If we are honest with ourselves, we realize the wonder of God's mercies. His mercies are reason 'enough'.

2) WE OFFER OURSELVES TO GOD AS A LIVING SACRIFICE (V. 1)

Paul said, "...*to offer your bodies as a living sacrifice, holy and pleasing to God*" (Rom. 12:1 NIV) expression "living sacrifice" is set against the backdrop of the Old Testament sacrifices. While the Old Testament worshipers offered an animal, New Testament worshipers offered themselves.

Just as the people of Israel presented their animal sacrifices to the priests, we are to hand over our bodies to God. We give ourselves to Him out of celebration for what God has done for us through his Son, Jesus Christ. When Paul uses the term body, he implies the whole person or the physical means, whereby the entire person is expressed. This presentation can be seen in much the same way that a defeated general of an army would hand over his sword to a conquering army, demonstrating the surrender of his whole being.

In this act of consecration, we don't give our dead bodies, but rather, we make a living sacrifice. A "living sacrifice" sounds like an oxymoron. A living sacrifice is more difficult to give than a dead sacrifice. A living sacrifice means something to us. It has the highest value. Dead sacrifices have no value. They don't mean anything to us. Living sacrifices cost us something. Dead sacrifices cost us nothing.

There were two "living sacrifices" recorded in the Bible. These two examples give us a clue about what it means to offer a living sacrifice. Both were acts of worship. The first was Isaac. He willingly put himself on the altar and would have died in obedience to God's will, but the Lord sent a ram to take his place. Isaac "died" just the same—he died to himself and willingly yielded to God's will. When he stepped off the altar, Isaac was a "living sacrifice." The second was Jesus. He was the perfect "living sacrifice" because he died as a sacrifice in obedience to God's will. But aren't you thankful that Jesus rose from the dead? Because He lives, we live.

The story is told of an old pastor in a little Scottish church who was asked to resign because not one person had made a commitment to Christ that whole year. Not one was saved; there were no conversions in the church for an entire year.

"When the old preacher said, "It has been a lean year, but there was one."

"One conversion?" asked an elder, "Who was it?"

"It was little Bobbie," replied the pastor.

They had forgotten the young boy who had not only been saved but had given himself in total consecration to God. "Little Bobbie" asked the usher to put the plate on the floor in a missionary meeting when somebody passed the plate for the offering. He stepped into it barefoot, saying, "I'll give myself—I have nothing else to give." Little Bobbie became the world-renowned minister Robert Moffatt, who, along with David Livingstone, gave his life to healing the open sores of the continent of Africa.

A woman asked her pastor, "What does it mean to be a living sacrifice?" Holding out a blank sheet of paper, the pastor replied, "It is to sign your name at the bottom of this blank sheet and let God fill it in the rest as he wills."

Paul had this very thing in mind when he instructed the Roman church "to offer your bodies as living sacrifices." That is what Robert Moffatt did. That is what is expected of each worshiper.

3) WE OFFER OURSELVES TO GOD ALL THE TIME

Living implies life, and life is an everyday experience. Offering ourselves to God should not be contained within a ninety-minute worship service. A living sacrifice is a sacrifice that is alive and continually in action. Worship occurs not just in the sanctuary but in our whole World. This means that worship moves away from just this hour and a half to all the hours of our lives. It moves away from one activity of coming to worship--to all of our activities: each relationship, task, opportunity, problem, success, and failure.

True worship is our personal linking of faith and works, the offering of our everyday lives to God. It isn't something that takes place only in church. Real worship sees the whole World as the temple of the living God and every ordinary day and deed as an act of worship.

Real worship is the offering of everyday life to God. We could say, "I am going to church to worship God," but we should also be able to say, "I am going to the office, or to the school, or to the garage, the garden, or the field, to worship God."

If you really want to know who and how you worship, let people see you in your office, hear you speak in your business affairs, see how you treat your neighbors, and see how you earn your money, save it, and spend it. Worship affects everything we do and everywhere we are, and everyone is watching.

I think that we have developed a kind of selective Christianity that allows us to be deeply and sincerely involved in worship and church activities. But if we are not careful, we can be very ungodly in our daily lives. And what is even sadder is that if we are not careful, most of us will not even realize it.

Worship is not just a church activity; it is a life activity. Worship is not a one-time thing; it is an all-the-time thing. Worship is not a once-a-week event.

A.W. Tozer said, "If you do not worship God seven days a week, you do not worship him on one day a week." [2]

It's a mistake to think that we must always go to a church building to worship. Let's not interpret worship as isolation and separation. True worship is offering God oneself and all that one does daily with it, wherever we might be.

I love what James Pike said, "When someone says "Oh, I can worship God anywhere," the question needs to be, "So do you?" [3]

4) WE OFFER OURSELVES TO GOD THROUGH TRANSFORMATION AND RENEWAL.

We demonstrate our commitment to God by refusing to conform to this World and being transformed through renewed minds. Paul stated, *"Do not be conformed to this world but be transformed by the renewing of your mind, so that you may prove what is that good, acceptable, and perfect will of God"* (Rom. 12:2 NKJV).

When we give ourselves to God, it reflects in how we live. As believers, we are in this World, but we are not to be trapped by it and molded by it. We are to live as holy people. People, who are distinct, separated from the ways of this World. We live as we do, not conforming to this World's patterns: people who are not chameleons or do not take their being and likeness from their surroundings. We live as transformed people. People who are changed are transformed on the inside.

Worshipping people are changed people. This is reflected in our walk, our talk, and our personality. When we give ourselves to God, we live not as self-centered but as Christ-centered lives. The World seeks to pressure our minds from the outside, but the person who has given themselves wholeheartedly to God allows God's Spirit to release His power from within.

That's what happens when Christ comes into a person's life. They become a new person; their mind is different; the mind of Christ is in them. Rather than allow the World to squeeze us into its mold, we allow Christ to shape us into his likeness. Worship is a molding process. We are to be to Christ what an image is to the original.

The primary goal of worship is transformation. The only way transformation can occur is to give ourselves totally to God so the mind and power of Jesus Christ can dwell in and through us. When that happens, we become more like Jesus in every moment and activity of our lives.

CONCLUSION

So my question for you and for me is: Are you ready, and am I ready, to put your whole self into God's plans? Are you ready to commit your all to Jesus?

The old saying goes, "Commitment is the giving of all one knows of himself to all one knows of God." Anything less than total commitment is unacceptable to God.

Finally, we offer ourselves up to God through transformation and renewal. I can honestly say that the World is trying to change our thinking into their thinking, but my friends, we have to stand up and be sure our thoughts are what God has destined for true believers.

I sometimes listen to old country songs on the radio. One singer talks about how people cancel out others if they don't like how they think. We see that every day in our current society. Our culture is trying to change how we feel by canceling our way of believing and living. I have lived 64 years and can decipher between a man and a woman. I can decipher between marriage for a man and woman that God ordained and between two males/two females marrying that God has not ordained. So, my friends, we must stand up for what God says in the Word, not what the World wants us to think or believe.

In today's world, I am heartbroken over these situations that we see as not being of God. Will I throw a wet washcloth in their faces? No, I will love them. It is only through the love of God that people can change and see that their ways are not God's ways.

You are today how you were treated as a child. If you were criticized as a child and taught that you are not good enough, you may feel unworthy to receive anything better than what you presently have. You may never reach out to gain more confidence if you feel lost and unconfident because of your upbringing. Open your hearts to Jesus, give Him your all, and watch what He does. You can't do it alone; let Him help you find yourself in Him.

You will do the right thing if your confidence and trust relies on God. Surround yourself with people who see your value, who say you are good at what you do, and those who love Jesus. Do not conform yourselves to negative thoughts others may tell you. Negativity is straight from Satan and will keep you from moving forward. Remember, we are only as good as we believe.

Believe in Jesus. We are all flawed as humans, but when you mess up, clean up with Jesus. My family did not drink while I grew up and attended church. As a teenager, I happened to work in a grocery store across the street from a rectory, and a priest I worked with at another local church asked me to run an errand with him to the store. He bought beer at the store and asked me to help him carry it to his church.

The priest buying beer confused me, so when I got home, I asked my mom, "Why does the priest drink beer, but we don't?" My mom stated, "We just don't". Then I asked, "How come my friends drink, but I can't"? Mom said, "What does your conscience say?" As I thought about what this meant, I realized our conscience is only as good as the foundation upon which somebody builds their life. Since my family didn't drink, my conscience told me I didn't need it to enjoy life. My teenage friends who came from families that did drink felt like it was okay, so they did.

To this day, I do believe drinking one beer on a special occasion does not mean a person is going to hell. However, suppose the devil can use this as a tool to get a stronghold on a person. In that case, that person may want additional beers on more occasions, and then drinking one beer becomes a slippery slope.

In my case, my conscience decided that not drinking at all is the best option for my life. If my conscience is built on the Word of God, I make better choices, no matter how the World tries to change my thinking. Apostle Paul says that our conscience is only as good as the foundation of God in our lives.

We need to understand that we are not perfect, but each day, as we follow Jesus, He shows us His mercy and faithfulness. When you mess up, clean up, for God is faithful to help us.

We are all flawed, but we can always be better. As a pastor, I am not perfect, but I serve a perfect God who died for us. The World is watching, and Jesus thanks you for following Him today. What does it mean to commit to following Jesus? *"This means that anyone who belongs to Christ has become a new person. The old life is gone, a new life has begun"*(2 Corinthians 5:17). I am a sinner, and Lord, I need you. I choose today to serve and commit my life to you. I want to grow in a relationship with you. I want You to be my God! Let God be your God.

♡ **Johnny and Debbie McDaniel** - *Pastor Duane is the most transparent, loving pastor I have ever known. I have learned so much from him about life, people, Jesus, and the Bible. I'm going to miss hearing his sermons.*

Pastor Duane has helped me become a better man, a better Christian, and an all-around better person. We have prayed a lot for each other over the years and will continue to pray for each other. Thank you, Duane, for being such a true friend. I love you and will miss you dearly. Please stay in touch.

Debbie and I wish both you and Gretchen a wonderful retirement. We will miss you and hope you return soon. Love and God Bless You Both, Johnny & Debbie McDaniel

♡ **Rich and Kathy White:** *We have appreciated Pastor Duane and Gretchen's ministry over the past eight years. Duane's preaching and teaching of God's*

Word has enriched our lives. Kathy still refers back to notes from the series on faith that he gave a few years ago. Rich particularly valued the "Shop Talk" of Men's Ministry, which Duane hosted at his shop. When Kathy was first diagnosed with colon cancer, Pastor Duane often telephoned to offer prayers and support. It meant so much to both of us. The pastor's transparency and humor have made the congregation connect with him.

Gretchen has been great in welcoming and greeting 'first timers' and 'old timers.' Many people may not realize her ministry of administration and bookkeeping skills that she faithfully performed weekly in the church office. Also, who could forget her marvelous cinnamon rolls? She was often found in the church kitchen organizing and preparing for various events. We will surely miss this precious couple and pray for the Lord's blessing on them as they transition into retirement. Rich and Kathy White.

CHAPTER 10

Pursuing God

THIS SUNDAY MORNING, LORD, WE are so thankful for you. We consider it a privilege to worship you in front of this congregation. This morning, I want to talk to you about pursuing God.

As you know, I am retiring after forty-one years of serving in the ministry. People have asked me, "If I had it to do all over again, would I do anything different?" My reply is, "No, I would not hesitate to do this all over again." I made a commitment to the Lord at the age of twenty-one after drifting away from the Lord for a few years.

When Gretchen and I were newly married in 1980 we immediately started working as youth sponsors and youth leaders at our Assembly of God church. The church was looking for youth sponsors, and even though we were not much older than them, we raised our hands to volunteer. When I decided to give my life to Jesus, I knew in my heart that I would never look back. I continued to work as a floor installer for ten years while we volunteered with the church youth. The youth pastor left a year later, and we continued working with the youth until I became a senior associate at the Assembly of God church in Silverton, Oregon.

Was it always easy? No! I told my floor installation boss that when the church can afford to pay me full-time, I will go there to work. I promised to give him a thirty-day notice so he had plenty of time to hire someone else. He leaned on the counter and looked at me inquisitively, "Why would you ever want to be a pastor?" I didn't hesitate to say, "Because I feel that is what God wants me to do." He said, "I think churches are good, except for one thing--there are people there."

A few months later, when the church offered me a full-time youth pastor job, I was excited to begin serving the Lord in this way. I earned $750 per month, two weeks of vacation per year, and no medical insurance. I was ready to start my new career.

Years later, I remember interviewing two seminary students who asked three questions: How many hours per week do I work, how much pay will I receive, and how much vacation time do I get? My first thought was, "Where is their heart to love people?" God gives pastors a special heart to love and care for people as their shepherds and leaders of the flock. Yes, sometimes we lead the sheep, and sometimes the sheep bite, but that is part of the ministry.

How would we like to end up by retirement? Simply said, "We would like to be pursuing God with everything we have in us".

I want to keep following God in everything He asked me to do. Remember the old 1977 television show, "Smokey and the Bandit," in hot pursuit every week? Before I was saved, I was a miserable young man feeling guilt and shame, with no peace. When I became saved, I wanted to pursue God with everything in me, just like Smokey and the Bandit. When I became truly committed to Jesus, I felt all the guilt and shame roll out of me. I felt brand new as Jesus set me free, forgiving me for my past sins. When this happened, there was a thirst in me for more righteousness. Pursuing God affected everything in my life. Our goal should 'be' to be more Christ-like. Will we ever be Jesus? No, but we can strive to be more like Him.

Our Lord helps us each day through the Holy Spirit. In Acts 1:8-11, Jesus told the apostles, *"But you will receive power when the Holy Spirit comes upon you. And you will be my witnesses, telling people about me everywhere—in Jerusalem, throughout Judea, in Samaria, and to the ends of the earth. After saying this, he was taken up into a cloud while they were watching, and they could no longer see him. As they strained to see him rising into heaven, two white-robed men suddenly stood among them. "Men of Galilee," they said, "why are you standing here staring into heaven? Jesus has been taken from you into heaven, but someday he will return from heaven in the same way you saw him go!"*

What a beautiful gift the Lord gave us when he ascended into heaven to send the gift of the Holy Spirit to reside within us. If we believe, our behaviors become more like Jesus. Remember, we can't walk without the Holy Spirit and the love of Jesus. As we pursue Jesus, Romans 12:2, "Don't *copy the behavior and customs of this world, but let God transform you into a new person by changing the way you think. Then you will learn to know God's will for you, which is good and pleasing and perfect.*"

We are to be transformed, not conformed to the patterns of this world. We see this happening every day in our lives. The news, self-interest groups, cultures, and society in general are trying to conform or change our Christian values into their way of thinking. Transformation is the societal process of changing an entire culture or civilization. Transformation can occur over several centuries and affect people slowly without them realizing a change is taking place.

Sanctification essentially means God is molding us, and the work God performs is an integral part of our salvation. In John 17:16-17, the Lord says, "*They are not of the world, even as I am not of it. Sanctify them by the truth; your word is truth*" (NIV). It is the same as growing in the Lord or spiritual maturity. Little by little, every day, those who are becoming more like Christ are becoming more sanctified.

Justification means being treated as righteous. The Bible states in several places that justification only comes through faith. Justification is not earned through our works; instead, we are covered by the righteousness of Jesus Christ. We are saved as a result of grace through faith. In Romans 5:1 it states, "*Therefore, since we have been justified through faith, we have peace with God through our Lord Jesus Christ*" (NIV). Once a person is justified, he needs nothing else to gain entrance into heaven.

As we pursue God, we begin to live a godly life. Godliness is an inward devotion toward God that is displayed outwardly toward people. Godliness shows in all my behaviors; if I am kind and loving, the attributes of Jesus' love are revealed. I sometimes fail, and the old ugly Duane raises his head. Where did that come from? I didn't see that one coming out of the blue, but unfortunately, it is in us. Satan is ready to rear his ugly voice when we least expect it. We battle with our minds every day.

Do we live 75%, 50% Godly? No, it is 100% Godly. When I was going through leukemia treatments, the doctors would give me a percentage of 25%

that I wouldn't make it and a 75% chance that I would live. The glass is a half-empty kind of diagnosis. Our doctors have the statistics, but we have God. We need to remember God is in control of our lives. The doctors told me ten years ago about the statistics and you know, after several clinical trials, chemotherapy, and other treatments, I am still here.

God has been faithful through all my challenges with leukemia, and we are grateful for what He has done. We praise the Lord and are thankful for what he continues to do, which is giving me more life. I am striving for a percentage of 100%. Proverbs 20:21 states, *"An inheritance obtained too early in life is not a blessing in the end."* I continue to strive for 100% until God reveals something different. I may not achieve 100%, but I will always strive for it.

What is God's purpose for our life? The Bible states in 1 Thessalonians 5:16-18, *"Always be joyful. Never stop praying. Be thankful in all circumstances, for this is God's will for you who belong to Christ Jesus."*

He says to be thankful in all circumstances. We may not feel grateful in all circumstances, but I am thankful to God. He sees the big picture, and we don't. We know the Lord, and He has a better plan for all of us than what we realize. In Psalms 30:5, we read, *"Weeping may last through the night, but joy comes in the morning."*

We should pursue in our lives, what areas we need to become more mature in. God wants to give us fresh dreams and purposes—we need community and each other. Pursuing is chasing after God. Listen to his promises for your life. Can you imagine the impact on society if we sought the Lord with all of our hearts? Can you imagine the change in our families, friends, and community?

In the Bible, David says in Psalm 139:23-24, *"Search me, O God, and know my heart; test me and know my anxious thoughts. Point out anything in me that offends you, and lead me along the path of everlasting life"*. To expand our purpose in life, we need to align ourselves with God.

1 Tim 6:11 states, *"But you, Timothy, are a man of God; so run from all these evil things. Pursue righteousness and a godly life, along with faith, love, perseverance, and gentleness."* If we don't cultivate these things in our lives, we become known for what we "oppose" instead of what we "propose." The

Christian community is getting hammered right now; we see it on the news. We have done it to ourselves. It just breaks my heart. If we were all tuned in to what God proposed for us, bow our knees, and surrender ourselves to Him, I believe God would respond to our nation's cry for help.

In the world today, we see all the different denominations. The world sees us as a big blob, not in sync with each other. We have churches with different beliefs, such as baptism techniques, how and when to take communion, and other procedures, which can confuse the world. In essence, all we need is a personal relationship with Jesus. When we reach heaven, He will straighten all this out for us.

Whoever calls on the name of the Lord will be saved. If we surrender our lives to him, heaven will be our home. In Matthew 5:13-16, Jesus says, *"You are the salt of the earth. But what good is salt if it has lost its flavor? Can you make it salty again? It will be thrown out and trampled underfoot as worthless. You are the light of the world—like a city on a hilltop that cannot be hidden. No one lights a lamp and then puts it under a basket. Instead, a lamp is placed on a stand, where it gives light to everyone in the house. In the same way, let your good deeds shine out for all to see, so that everyone will praise your heavenly Father."*

In other words, God has called us to be the "Shake and Shine." Our faith should do the same thing. Christianity should bring "flavor" and "shine" to our lives. People see you and want to be like you. What causes Christians to not freak out over daily news? Or be kind to someone angry with them? How do they do it? What do they have?

Salt is flavor, and light draws people out of darkness. Have you ever been in the dark with no flashlight? If one person has a flashlight in a dark cave, we follow the light. If you have the light of Jesus in you, people are drawn to you. Joy is serving Jesus. Does it mean that we will not have difficulties or troubles? Does it mean we will not have tears, pain, or frustrations? No. Light is intended to be seen, like a ship seeing the lighthouse, and the way is made clear.

God-like qualities: Righteousness, Godliness, Faith, Love and Gentleness. If you split the word righteousness in half, it means right/ness, which means "be right and do right." Having a heart that is good with God and having a heart available for God to recreate in you.

1. Through Jesus, Psalm 51:10 said, *"Create in me a clean heart, O God. Renew a loyal spirit within* me." This is living a lifestyle pleasing to God. A righteous person is one who lives according to God's guidance and shows the world through his actions. We condone a strong self-image, pursue what is right with God, and show man what is right.

2. Godliness lives in reverence and awe of God. Our whole lives should center under God. If we don't have the awe of God, we feel we can do what we want. All believers will appear before the Bema Seat of God in heaven to be judged on our faith–we have to stand before God someday. We live a life that God shows us. There needs to be an "awe" and reverence of God. Their whole life lives before God. Galatians 5:22 states, *"But the Holy Spirit produces this fruit in our lives: love, joy, peace, patience, kindness, goodness, faithfulness,"* and treat others well. Bad pastors can give Christianity a bad name. If a pastor does something immoral, they do not have an awe or reverence for God. We are to live our lives pleasing to God. Be kind to others, be faithful, and follow God. Be wise and be the fruits. Treat others with dignity.

3. Faith–loyalty to God, everything we do from birth to death. Be loyal to God. Be obedient, want to please, learn to trust and depend on him, grow in our faith, and be committed. It is the person who wants to please God in everything we do.

4. Dependability–can God count on you? When it comes down to it, can God count on you to be dependable and to follow Him? When I don't know what to do, I keep on doing what I know to do.

When my granddaughter died last summer in an accident, I didn't know what to tell my wife; I didn't know what to do with my son and his wife. I didn't know what to say to my other younger granddaughter. I was brokenhearted, crushed, and wounded, and I didn't know what to do. You know what I did? I continued to do what I was supposed to do, what I knew to do. I was honest. I asked God why. I had questions; it was a situation I hadn't walked through. I didn't know what to do. I wasn't mad; I just kneeled and prayed.

After three weeks, we returned from the memorial, and the staff said I needed to preach. The congregation needs to know you are okay; I can't be fake with my feelings because I didn't know what to do. So I did what I knew to do: to be honest with my feelings. I asked why? Why God? I knew what I should do: pray, talk to God, listen to God, sing to God, turn to God, and surrender to God. I wasn't mad at God or disappointed; I didn't know what to do. In my surrendering, God was there, and I have complete faith that I will see my granddaughter again when I get to heaven. In ICU, I whispered in my granddaughter's ear, "I will see you in a few minutes." Why? Because I know the Lord says, a thousand years is a day, and a day is a thousand years. When we see our loved ones in heaven, they will not say what took you so long; they will say, Hi, I just got here, and it is nice that you are here already. Understand that God is outside of time and space.

1. Love--agape love. Agape love involves faithfulness, commitment, and an act of the will. God loves us with an unfailing love. I want God's best love. We need to care for others unconditionally and be willing to listen. I want God's best for other people.

2. Endurance--We should move closer to the Lord. We need strength and balance, and the snail reaches the ark by endurance. The Christian life is a *journey*, not a 100-yard dash.

3. Gentleness—We should live with gentle discipline, not weakness, but meekness and humility. Matthew 11:29 says, *"Take my yoke upon you. Let me teach you, because I am humble and gentle at heart, and you will find rest for your souls."*

4. Love other people and desire a peaceful lifestyle. Pursue time with God. Do it intently and with purpose. I love singing the old hymn:

> I need Thee, oh, I need Thee
> Every hour, I need Thee;
> Oh, bless me now, my Savior,
> I come to Thee.

Let it be our prayer: we need you; today, we need you desperately; we need you to work in our families, in our communities, in our state, and in our nations. I pray this prayer for this day. This day, we say we need you, and every hour, we need you. I pray that we can navigate through the trials of this day. Keep our eyes on you. I pray you grant every need today. Make a difference with people. Bless each person today. If there is someone who hasn't surrendered your life to Jesus, you can do that right now. Maybe you are tired of doing everything yourself. He will be there for you. I need Jesus today.

Dear Lord Jesus, I need you. I surrender my heart; I ask you to forgive me of my sins, to come into my life and help me today. Lord, you promised to walk through my trials with me, and I commit my life to you today in Jesus' Name. Amen. If you prayed this today, you are a new creation in Jesus. Go with Jesus; He is with us every step of the way.

"Seek the Kingdom of God above all else, and live righteously,
and he will give you everything you need"

— (Matthew 6:33).

♡ *Mike and Belinda West: When we moved to Redmond three years ago, this was the fifth church we had visited. When we left church that day, we knew Redmond Assembly of God would be our church home. What delighted us the most was that Pastor Duane came down to the pews after the service to welcome us. I noticed he did this after every service. The following Sunday, we were impressed that Pastor Duane remembered our names and even took us to lunch to social-ize and get to know us better. He is definitely a people's pastor. We wish you and Gretchen a wonderful retirement. Mike and Belinda West*

CHAPTER 11

Understanding Contentment

Happy New Year! I want to wish every one of you a delightful new year. It is amazing how fast each year goes by. You know how we make those New Year resolutions each year to lose weight, exercise more, and be nicer to our family. We say it will be a better year if we pray more, read the Bible more, and attend church every Sunday. In reality, most of the time we spend worrying about our children and how they will turn out; we worry about our money and how we will pay the bills; and we worry about work and our unpredictable health. If that isn't enough to worry about, we take on the government, elections, and the global wars among the nations. It is no wonder why we all may feel a little anxious.

Some people wanting to get rid of their worries may even receive a word from the Lord to move to a different house or another State for new scenery and a new start on life. They spend weeks preparing to sell their home, pack up all their belongings, and finally, the big day arrives to stuff everything they own into a massive 26-foot U-Haul. The last things to go in are "all their problems" as they say their goodbyes to family and friends. They secure and latch the U-Haul doors so all the problems are locked safely inside.

As they excitedly travel down the road, taking in the new scenery, it feels like a fresh start in life. After all, the scenery and house are different, and the new job looks promising. They dream of their new life with excitement and anticipation without any problems because they have left them all behind.

As they back up the U-Haul into their new driveway and unlatch the doors, all their problems come stumbling out to greet them face-to-face. Their face drops as they realize their issues followed them to their new home.

Apostle Paul says, *"Don't worry about anything; instead pray about everything. Tell God what you need, and thank him for all he has done. Then you will experience God's peace, which exceeds anything we can understand. His peace will guard your hearts and minds as you live in Christ Jesus"* (Philippians 4:6-7).

Sometimes, it is hard to be content with what God gives us. Understanding what the word 'contentment' means is a source of satisfaction. The word means to be contented, satisfied, and peaceful with what you have, where you live, and what God has given you. So many of us yearn for 'more,' a more prominent place, more money, a newer car, or more play time. The World teaches us to be unsatisfied and always strive for more, but Jesus says in Romans 12:2,"*Don't copy the behavior and customs of this World, but let God transform you into a new person by changing the way you think. Then you will learn to know God's will for you, which is good and pleasing and perfect."*

Contentment means to be happy with today and the present moment because that is all we have. As Pastor Duane pauses and reflects, he says the present moment is the only moment we have with our spouse, children, family, grandchildren, and friends. Living in the present is true contentment. True contentment is at this very moment. I don't have to worry because I have everything I need and I don't need anything else. It is easy to be content on Sunday morning; you see your friends, talk warmly to everyone, and feel the Holy Spirit move when the worship music starts to play, and then you hear a great message about God and how He works in your life. But, if your husband walked out on you, or you hear from your doctor, "I'm sorry, you have six months to live, or someone you love has passed away, then it is very difficult to be content."

In the Bible, Paul says in Philippians 4:10-14, *"How I praise the Lord that you are concerned about me again. I know you have always been concerned for me, but you didn't have the chance to help me. Not that I was ever in need, for I have learned how to be content with whatever I have. I know how to live on almost nothing or with everything. I have learned the secret of living in every situation, whether it is with a full stomach or empty, with plenty or little. For I can do every-thing through Christ, who gives me strength. Even so, you have done well to share with me in my present difficulty."*

As Paul in the Bible states, I have learned how to be content with whatever I have. I believe God is more glorified when we are in our trials. We must wean ourselves from our children as they grow up and teach them how they should go. God is trying to wean us from the World by loving the treasures we store up in Heaven, glorifying our Lord. Happiness is not from our circumstances. Contentment comes from God. Being around people who are happy and content with their lives is so pleasurable. Being content all the time is easy to say, but hard to do.

Contentment is internal satisfaction, which does not demand changes in external circumstances. Believers can be content no matter what the outward circumstances. Believers are content to know Jesus and depend on His grace. He is a good, good Father.[1]

I have learned the secret of living in every situation, whether it is with a full stomach or an empty one, with abundance or having little, for I can do everything through Christ, who gives me strength. In every difficulty, the Lord gives me the strength I need each moment of each day.

The Lord has promised to be with us and never leave us. We have that promise to carry around with us when life becomes difficult or challenging. There is stuff bigger than us: If I call President Biden, do I believe he would answer? No, not really. I would be shocked if he did. But, if the press secretary put my call through and said, "Duane is on the phone, Mr. President," I would be extremely shocked. This action is so much bigger than what I believed possible. It is the same with God. He is so almighty, powerful, and more extensive than we can visualize and think with our puny brains. Yet, when we cry out to Him, reach out to Him, and call on Him, He is there if we believe it is possible.

We have to believe and have confidence that everything works for good and never 'doubt' God. In Romans 8:28, Paul states, *"And we know that God causes everything to work together for the good of those who love God and are called according to his purpose for them."*

How does God think? Are we willing to let God be God? Sometimes, we ask, "If God loves me, why did this just happen?" Our terrible trials create our questions. The word "fear not" appears 365 times in the Bible. Every day, we have fears about something.

Publicly, we fear where our government is going. Privately, we have fear about how our kids are going to turn out, if we have enough money to pay bills and pay for emergencies, if our car is going to operate so we can drive to work, if our health is going to hold up so we can support our family, or worse, will it hold up so I don't die. The opposite of fear is love, not faith. Love the Lord--the Lord loves each of us. We can't blame God for things that happen--it is not His fault.

Psalms 71:1-2 states, *"O Lord, I have come to you for protection; don't let me be disgraced. Save me and rescue me, for you do what is right. Turn your ear to listen to me and set me free."* We need to be willing to let God BE GOD in our lives. Do we put our trust and confidence in Him, or do we try to figure out life ourselves?

Let me never be put to shame or confusion, for as Joshua 1:9 says, *"This is my command--be strong and courageous! Do not be afraid or discouraged. For the Lord your God is with you wherever you go."*

Riches can ruin the soul; people in poverty are closer to God because they have to trust God for every morsel of food, a warm and safe place to sleep, and a few dollars to buy what they need to eat or stay clean.

There is a movie called Cool Running. Four Jamaicans form their countries first-ever bobsled team to compete in the 1988 Winter Olympics. The other teams treated them as outsiders, who feared they would only embarrass the sport by competing, saying they could never be happy winning a gold medal. One Jamaican bobsled participant said, "If you are never happy without a gold medal, you won't be happy with one." It is so true that unhappy people are unhappy about almost everything. They are not content in life. If a person is always looking forward to the next happy event like a vacation, the summer, the kids going to college, the next paycheck, or retirement, they never find happiness in the present.

Why do some people prosper, and why do some people just never seem to get a break? God has a purpose for it. With our limited "knot hole" view in the fence, we can't see the perspective God sees as he looks down and sees what needs to happen next. The World does not revolve around us, but God sees the whole picture, which is good, pleasing, and perfect.

In Philippians 4:12, it is paraphrased that I have learned to be content in every situation. Nothing happens by chance, but everything is ordained by God, the good, the bad, and the ugly. He is Our God, and we are not.

From our point of view, everything looks random, but everything is in divine order. Proverbs 16:33 states, "*We may throw the dice, but the Lord determines how they fall.*" God determines what happens in life, and many times, we don't understand it, especially something that hurts us, like the death of a loved one. We must surrender every ounce of our being, surrender our lives fully, and ask Him to give us strength. We need to ask Him to get us through by His will, not ask Him to provide us with what we want. We need to surrender and let Jesus take the wheel.

Finally, we have to learn and experience that Jesus is enough. Jesus heals, gives us strength, protects us, loves us, and resides in you and me. Be content wherever you are and have peace and contentment. I love and rely on the Lord in everything I do. God is enough for me. Everything I need is in you, Lord. Yes, we are human and flawed, and we can easily forget and start worrying and fretting again, but remember, are you willing to let God be God?"

"The Lord is my shepherd; I have all that I need"

— (Psalm 23:1).

♡ **Shirley Jackson**: *I want you both to know how much of a blessing you have been to me. I have been coming to Redmond Assembly of God since 2012 and am thankful to have been under your leadership. Gretchen, I want to say you are such a wonderful example of a good Christian woman. I know God has many good things in store for you both, and I am excited to see them fulfilled. Lots of love and prayers, Shirley.*

CHAPTER 12
The Golden Rule

IN THE PAST, WE HAVE talked about contentment. It is not about what we have or want, but knowing God's hand is upon us. Whether we are having bad times or good times, lean times or abundant times, we realize that God has His hand on us at all times. I am grateful for that today, and I trust that you are thankful for that, too.

Today, we are going to talk about the golden rule. The passage I am going to share with you is Matthew 7:7-12:

>*⁷Keep on asking, and you will receive what you ask for. Keep on seeking, and you will find. Keep on knocking, and the door will be opened to you.*

>*⁸For everyone who asks, receives. Everyone who seeks, finds. And to everyone who knocks, the door will be opened.*

>*⁹You parents—if your children ask for a loaf of bread, do you give them a stone instead?*

>*¹⁰Or if they ask for a fish, do you give them a snake? Of course not!*

>*¹¹So if you sinful people know how to give good gifts to your children, how much more will your heavenly Father give good gifts to those who ask Him?*

¹²*Do to others whatever you would like them to do to you. This is the essence of all that is taught in the law and the prophets.*

The 'golden rule' is something that occurs constantly in our lives. We all have heard of it: **'Do unto others as you would want them to do unto you.**

There is this legalistic student who always wanted to do everything by scripture. He wanted to do it only if it was in 'the book.' He wanted everything in his life to be legal and by the rules. One day, he met this girl at college and wanted to start dating her. They dated a few times, and one night, as they walked to the dormitory, he felt like he would like to kiss her but struggled, in his mind, with what it says in scripture, so he just said 'goodnight.'

Each night, as he walked her back to her dormitory, he kept struggling with how he could kiss her and not disobey God. Again, he starts to say goodnight, and she reaches over to him, plants a huge kiss on his mouth, and stays there for a minute. He is flabbergasted by such a passionate kiss, and all he can say is, "Scripture, scripture, oh, what scripture applies to this?" She wittingly says, "Do unto others as you would want them to do unto you."

The golden rule has always been popular. In Matthew 7:7, it states, *"Keep on asking, and you will receive what you ask for. Keep on seeking, and you will find. Keep on knocking, and the door will be opened to you. "*This sums up that we need to believe and ask, and we will receive what we ask for. We do have to be careful what we ask for.

I am thankful for God's grace and mercy. Jesus, we thank you for your love, grace, and mercy.

We need to use these words as we navigate through life and watch what is happening in the world today. In our day-to-day lives, we need to highlight mercy and grace. Sometimes, we find ourselves a little short-tempered, and we must ensure our attitudes are right. By spending quiet time with God, the Lord will help us through each day. We take our thoughts captive, saying we will not mistreat anyone today; we will control our temper and practice being patient with others.

In Luke 24:49, Jesus says, *"And now I will send the Holy Spirit, just as my Father promised. But stay here in the city until the Holy Spirit comes and fills you with power from heaven."* Jesus is always with us and also within us. He sent the Holy Spirit to come and fill us with power from the heavenly Father.

We need to direct our attitudes toward the Holy Spirit and our good attitudes toward our children. As parents, we don't give our kids everything they want; just like God doesn't give us everything we want. He is a good, good Father. He gives us what is best for us, just like we do with our children.

God has our best interests at heart. Jesus challenges us to love others as he loves us. We need to treat others in the same way God loves us. Remember, the golden rule is ***"Do to others whatever you would like them to do to you"***(Matthew 7:12).

You know, sometimes we all go through trials and struggles. I believe God allows us to go through things that we really don't want to go through. When bad things happen, it is not God's fault, and He isn't doing it "to us" but He is allowing us to go through these trials. James says to be joyful in the trials as God strengthens us. God allows us to undergo trials here on earth to shape our character and faith.

In Him, we need to trust more and turn to Him for every emotional need. We need to love others and show people God's love. We need to show generosity toward others. Be generous, not just with finances, but with our daily time, words, and actions. Show mercy and grace to others. The Lord wants us to show other people the great love He has inside for each of us. The golden rule sums up the apostles: Love, love God, and love others. Jesus showed us His love by dying on the cross for us and forgiving us for our sins.

In Matthew 22:36-39 when Jesus was asked this question, *"Teacher, which is the most important commandment in the law of Moses?* Jesus replied, *"You must love the* LORD *your God with all your heart, all your soul, and all your mind. This is the first and greatest commandment. A second is equally important: 'Love your neighbor' as yourself."*

We are dealing with this in our culture today. We, as a society, are not generally nice to each other. Social media permits us to make hateful comments because we are not face-to-face with that person. With less respect for authority, lawlessness takes hold because there is no discipline or fatherly love to show right and wrong. When you take criminal discipline away, criminals are left to run wild without fear of arrest or discipline.

The Golden Rule has love as its driving force. Romans 13:8 states, *"Owe nothing to anyone—except for your obligation to love one another. If you love your neighbor, you will fulfill the requirements of God's law."* There are commandments on adultery, stealing, lying, and honoring your father and mother, because love is the fulfillment of the law. There are people you are close to every day at work, church, or family and friends. We love these people. If we show people we love them, they usually return that love.

A common misquote of Matthew 7:12 is **Do unto others as they do unto you**. The Lord says, ***"Do to others whatever you would like them to do to you"****(Matthew 7:12).

There is a vast difference between these two sentences. It means, "If you are unkind to me, I will be kind to you; if you invite me to dinner, I will ask you to dinner; if you say something mean, I will not be mean to you. The Golden Rule is not to pay back for wronged actions. The Bible says, *"Do not take revenge, my dear friends, but leave room for God's wrath, for it is written: "It is mine to avenge; I will repay," says the Lord"* (Romans 12:19 NIV).

If someone wrongs us Luke 6:27 (NIV) says, *"But to you who are willing to listen, I say, love your enemies! Do good to those who hate you."* Learn to love your enemies and pray for those who mistreat you. Sometimes, we read that scripture and say, "I don't like that scripture, but the Lord is right". Turn the other cheek and go the extra mile; what credit is it for you if you love those who love you? If you pay back something, what credit is it for you? The reward is great when you follow what the Lord says. With all my heart, we should be looking for opportunities to be nice to people who are not friendly to us.

This morning, I pulled out of my driveway. I live about five miles out in the country from the church. There is snow on the roads, and I am driving following this car going 28 miles per hour. Yes, there is snow on the road, but this guy is pokey. I follow on his tail, thinking I can pass him at some point, but the opportunity doesn't present itself. I then find myself getting a little impatient as I have to be at the church to stream this message, and my natural impatience comes when I realize I may not have enough time to run by and get my McDonald's coffee. I thought that this guy might be older, and I got frustrated. Why am I in an uproar about this? I decided not to pass him because if I went around him and scared him, it could cause an accident. I ask myself again, "Why am I so impatient?" Is coffee at McDonald's that important? If I am five minutes late to church, streaming will start five minutes late. Passing this older man on the highway is not worth it. I must love him and be considerate of what he is experiencing. Maybe he hasn't driven on the snow very much and is scared to death. I am not going to endanger his life to get my needs met.

To avoid these types of situations, we need to use wisdom. The answer is that we have a choice to make a good decision. When I was a kid, my dad would say that if I came home with a black eye, society says, 'hit them back', but Jesus said something different. We can go through life without paying back everyone for every hurt. Jesus didn't just say it. He lived it.

During his thirty-three years on earth, people treated Jesus unkindly; they mocked him when He talked, they turned Him away, and people failed to believe He is the son of God. He was ridiculed, taunted, and abused, but He didn't come out of his godly character. We need to put on His righteousness, not self-righteousness.

The same power Jesus sent to us in the form of the Holy Spirit is the same power Jesus had on earth. When we are born again, the Holy Spirit resides inside us. We need to be different as believers. By believing in Jesus, we need to heed the call to follow Him.

What impact does this have on us? Some people might think of us as weak, as people of God. People saw this in Jesus, too. But they also saw his goodness, how he talked and treated people, and his kindness toward everyone. As believers, we can show our light to non-believers by acting like Jesus. We can be friendly and kind to others, offer encouraging words, treat all people respectfully, and show them our light in Jesus. Like everyone else, sometimes I don't feel like Jesus, and this is where we have to put our trust in God and the Holy Spirit. He wants to work in us for His good pleasure and to show others his love for us.

So let me give you one other variation of the golden rule, "**Don't do to others what you don't want done to you.** If you don't want to be stolen from, don't steal from them.

The story of the 'Parable of the Good Samaritan' in Luke 13:30-37 describes, "*A Jewish man was traveling from Jerusalem down to Jericho, and he was attacked by bandits. They stripped him of his clothes, beat him up, and left him half dead beside the road. By chance a priest came along. But when he saw the man lying there, he crossed to the other side of the road and passed him by. A Temple assistant walked over and looked at him lying there, but he also passed by on the other side.*"

³³"*Then a despised Samaritan came along, and when he saw the man, he felt compassion for him.* ³⁴*Going over to him, the Samaritan soothed his wounds with olive oil and wine and bandaged them. Then he put the man on his own donkey and took him to an inn, where he took care of him.* ³⁵*The next day he handed the innkeeper two silver coins, telling him, take care of this man. If his bill runs higher than this, I'll pay you the next time I'm here.*"

³⁶"*Now which of these three would you say was a neighbor to the man who was attacked by bandits?*" Jesus asked.

³⁷The man replied, "*The one who showed him mercy.*" Then Jesus said, "*Yes, now go and do the same.*"

Your neighbor is everyone, including your enemy. Love your enemies. It is so important to put yourself in other people's shoes. The royal law is to love your neighbor as yourself. You are doing right. The care and concern we have for ourselves is what we give to others.

He doesn't want us to think we are better than others. He wants to love others. Better you than me is not a good attitude either. We need to build each other up and encourage others. Let the words we speak to others allow them to stand firm, not knock them down. When people are struggling or feeling hurt, they don't need someone to cut them down, hurt them, or give advice. They need your love, support, and Jesus' love—people to uphold them and strengthen their hearts and minds. We are to help them.

I have dealt with leukemia for years. The Cancer Center staff has such great spiritual gifts. They have a heart to help each of us as we struggle with the fight for life. They have a heart to see people well. You sit in those infusion rooms, three times per week every 27 days. I would listen to people who were sick. When people hurt, they hurt people. I could hear these hurting people hurting the staff. I would pray for them. Even going through difficult times, we can always encourage others, change our attitude, and give life to others. We believe in Jesus and know He loved people who needed healing and kindness.

We are going to face people who are experiencing difficulties. You may face your challenges with health, children, marriages, or finances. Whatever you are going through put it at the foot of the cross. He wants us to be lifters, strengtheners, and positive in life. Look for people this week to encourage and help. Ask your Holy Spirit to give you the insight to listen with an open ear to people you are talking to and see how you can help by supporting, encouraging, or just loving them. God gave us two ears to listen and hear what others are saying. Can you hear beyond the words they are saying? You can pray for them quietly.

There is always hope in Jesus. Your presence is always with us. May we live by the golden rule that you have given us that we would love others as we would have others love us. There is a lot of chaos and stress in the world today, but we can overcome it by giving everything to Jesus at the foot of the cross.

We can trust Him and I love singing this hymn about trusting Jesus:

Tis so sweet to trust in Jesus,
and to take him at his word;
just to rest upon his promise,
and to know, "Thus saith the Lord."

Jesus, Jesus, how I trust him!
How I've proved him o'er and o'er!
Jesus, Jesus, precious Jesus!
O for grace to trust him more!

♡ **Ryan and Jennifer Acree:** *We love hearing Pastor Duane's sermons on biblical topics. Pastor Duane actually married us twice, once officially at Redmond Assembly of God and another time at our wedding venue. Ryan and I actually met each other at Redmond Assembly of God and ten months later, we married. Pastor Duane and Gretchen will always have a special place in our hearts. Congratulations on your retirement! Ryan & Jennifer*

CHAPTER 13

Facing Impossible Situations

DURING OUR LIFETIME, ALL OF US have had to face impossible situations. Perhaps it was a terminal cancer diagnosis, loss of a job when you desperately needed the income, loss of your home, or the unexpected loss of a loved one. In the middle of difficult situations, our emotions run high and we may feel doubt that we can climb out. We doubt whether anyone or even God can solve or help us out of our impossible situation.

In the Bible, Moses was susceptible to doubt. He had led the Israelites out of Egypt and this was their first taste of freedom in over 400 years. Moses was troubled as the people angrily complained about their hardship of not having meat to eat. They complained that they never see anything but manna; where is the fish we ate in Egypt?

In Numbers 11:1-23, it states, *"Soon the people began to complain about their hardship, and the LORD heard everything they said. Then the LORD's anger blazed against them, and he sent a fire to rage among them, and he destroyed some of the people in the outskirts of the camp. ²Then the people screamed to Moses for help, and when he prayed to the LORD, the fire stopped. ³After that, the area was known as Taberah (which means "the place of burning"), because fire from the LORD had burned among them there.*

⁴Then the foreign rabble who were traveling with the Israelites began to crave the good things of Egypt. And the people of Israel also began to complain. "Oh, for some meat!" they exclaimed. ⁵"We remember the fish we used to eat for free in Egypt. And we had all the cucumbers, melons, leeks, onions, and garlic we wanted. ⁶*But now our appetites are gone. All we ever see is this manna!"*

⁷*The manna looked like small coriander seeds, and it was pale yellow like gum resin.* ⁸*The people would go out and gather it from the ground. They made flour by grinding it with hand mills or pounding it in mortars. Then they boiled it in a pot and made it into flat cakes. These cakes tasted like pastries baked with olive oil.* ⁹*The manna came down on the camp with the dew during the night.*

¹⁰*Moses heard all the families standing in the doorways of their tents whining, and the* Lord *became extremely angry. Moses was also very aggravated.* ¹¹*And Moses said to the* Lord, *"Why are you treating me, your servant, so harshly? Have mercy on me! What did I do to deserve the burden of all these people?* ¹²*Did I give birth to them? Did I bring them into the world? Why did you tell me to carry them in my arms like a mother carries a nursing baby? How can I carry them to the land you swore to give their ancestors?* ¹³*Where am I supposed to get meat for all these people? They keep whining to me, saying, 'Give us meat to eat!'* ¹⁴*I can't carry all these people by myself! The load is far too heavy!* ¹⁵*If this is how you intend to treat me, just go ahead and kill me. Do me a favor and spare me this misery!"*

¹⁶*Then the* Lord *said to Moses, "Gather before me seventy men who are recognized as elders and leaders of Israel. Bring them to the Tabernacle to stand there with you.* ¹⁷*I will come down and talk to you there. I will take some of the Spirit that is upon you, and I will put the Spirit upon them also. They will bear the burden of the people along with you, so you will not have to carry it alone.*

¹⁸*"And say to the people, 'Purify yourselves, for tomorrow you will have meat to eat. You were whining, and the* Lord *heard you when you cried, "Oh, for some meat! We were better off in Egypt!" Now the* Lord *will give you meat, and you will have to eat it.* ¹⁹*And it won't be for just a day or two, or for five or ten or even twenty.* ²⁰*You will eat it for a whole month until you gag and are sick of it. For you have rejected the* Lord, *who is here among you, and you have whined to him, saying, "Why did we ever leave Egypt?"'"*

²¹*But Moses responded to the* Lord, *"There are 600,000 foot soldiers here with me, and yet you say, 'I will give them meat for a whole month!'* ²²*Even if we butchered all our flocks and herds, would that satisfy them? Even if we caught all the fish in the sea, would that be enough?"*

[23]*Then the* LORD *said to Moses, "Has my arm lost its power? Now you will see whether or not my word comes true!"*

Moses had some insurmountable challenges, and we are going to confront situations in our lives that look impossible. Moses had an impossible situation. Moses had a miraculous exodus from Egypt and had been through a lot. Even as a baby he had been a "basket case." Moses led the Israelites across the Sinai Peninsula to the Eastern arm of the Red Sea. There they were stopped by the sea. Pharaoh and the Egyptian Army gave pursuit gaining on Moses. The Israelites and Moses were pinned down between the mountains and the sea.

Moses prayed for God's help. God sent a column of fire to keep the Egyptians from advancing all night. God then opened the Red Sea, holding back great walls of water, and the Israelites passed through the sea to the other side. Eventually, the Egyptians tried to cross too, but were drowned when God allowed the waters to return to their original place.

Certainly this would be the end of Moses' troubles, right? No, not hardly! Moses' challenges were just starting. Moses soon found he had an even bigger challenge to face than the Egyptians—a challenge that would not go away, but he had to face every day for 40 years or 14,610 days.

What a seemingly impossible situation? He was responsible for feeding the three and half million Israelites and caring for all their needs. Something as simple as water to drink was a big deal. The volume necessary to satisfy the thirst of the Israelites and their cattle is estimated at 20,000,000 gallons for ONE DAY! Where do you find that amount of water in the desert?

Firewood used in cooking the food would take 4,000 tons of wood for ONE DAY.

And, then there is food. Can you imagine the amount of food it took to feed three and half million people? Moses would need 2,500 tons, or five million pounds of food each day.

But then another problem: Each time they camped, a campground two-thirds the size of the State of Rhode Island was required, or a total of 750 square miles. Just think of how much space they needed for nightly camping.

Do you think Moses figured all this out before he left Egypt? I think not! Moses was trusting God to take care of all these things.

So when the Israelites said they wanted to have a daily diet of meat—out in the Sinai desert where hardly any vegetation grows for even a goat to survive—Moses couldn't get his head around how he was going to do it. Was this too big for God? It was such a staggering and long-term problem that even Moses, who had, in the past, seen God send ten plaques against Egypt, and watched God open the Red Sea—couldn't see how this could happen.

Some situations bogle our minds, attempt us to doubt our faith. God may have done many things for us in the past, but suddenly, we are faced with something so new and so intimidating that our faith balks at the possibility God can pull this one off.

God challenged Moses' unbelief in verse Numbers11:23, "Has my arm lost its power?" Other translations say, "Is this beyond the Lord's reach?"(NABRE); "So, do you think I can't take care of you?" (MSG); and "Am I not strong enough?" (NIV)

Aren't you thankful, we serve a God who hasn't lost His power? Whose power knows no limits! Who is able to perform ANYTHING He promises, no matter how impossible it seems.

The question remains for many people, "How do we know God's power will help us?" There are mighty forces God has implemented to aid us. None of these forces have been retracted to this day.

Here are six of them:

1) THE BLOOD OF JESUS HAS NEVER LOST ITS POWER

In 1 Peter 1:18-20 (NIV) it states, *"For you know that it was not with perishable things such as silver or gold that you were redeemed from the empty way of life handed down to you from your ancestors, but with the precious blood of Christ, a lamb without blemish or defect."*

The blood of Christ is called 'precious'. Why? Because you must remember, the Blood of Jesus is the most valuable substance in our universe. The Blood of Jesus alone can dissolve your sin.

In Isaiah 1:18..."*Though your sins are like scarlet, I will make them as white as snow. Though they are red like crimson, I will make them as white as wool.*" God's hand is not shortened because the Blood of Jesus never LOST its power!

2) THE HOLY SPIRIT HASN'T BEEN WITHDRAWN

Some will say the Age of Miracles is past; that the Holy Spirit can't do the same things today that He did in the Book of Acts. I am here to challenge that notion.

What was the Holy Spirit given for in Acts 1:8? What was God's purpose? To give us POWER to WITNESS to the world. Have we finished with our assignment yet? No!

Joel's prophecy quoted by Peter in Acts 2 states, that the Holy Spirit will continue to be poured out until He comes back for His church—until that... "*great and glorious Day of the Lord*" (Acts 2:20).

Since the Holy Spirit is with us now, His power is still available to us. All things are possible with God! The miraculous can happen at any moment if we reach out and claim it by faith.

3) JESUS CONQUERED ALL SPIRITUAL POWERS

In Colossians 2:15 it says, "*In this way, he disarmed the spiritual rulers and authorities. He shamed them publicly by his victory over them on the cross.*"

What looked like a defeat for the Son of God in the physical realm became the utter defeat of the Prince of Darkness in the spiritual realm. You might say that in killing Jesus, the devil defeated himself. Then Jesus rose, but the devil couldn't recover.

The Message Bible states in Colossians 2:15, "*He stripped all the spiritual tyrants in the universe of their sham authority at the Cross and marched them naked through the streets.*"

Jesus is Lord of Heaven, Lord of Earth, and of all under the earth. In 1 John 4:4 it explains, "*...because He who is in you is greater than he who is in the world*" (NKJV).

4) JESUS CHRIST IS STILL THE SAME: YESTERDAY, TODAY, AND FOREVER

Sometimes we can't see God when our problems look so big or they have gone on for a long time. If God is involved, the circumstances don't matter. The circumstances do not change God's ability to help you.

The good news is that God has not changed. Hebrews 13:8 states, *"Jesus Christ is the same yesterday, today and forever."* His nature as our greatest advocate has not changed and never will.

Miracles are natural to God. In Scripture we read, *"You are the God who performs miracles; you display your power among the peoples"* (Psalm 77:14 NIV).

Miracles are still necessary today because there is still a human need. God triumphs by the smallest of things and in the biggest of things. God still intervenes, changing the natural course of events in answer to believing prayer. It is still true that all things are possible with God through prayer.

5) GOD'S WORD DOES NOT RETURN VOID

"So shall My word be that goes forth from My mouth, it shall not return to Me void, but it shall accomplish what I please. And it shall prosper in the thing for which I sent it" (Isaiah 55:11 NKJV).

The Bible may look like other books, but it is not. The words of the Bible are ALIVE. They are words with spiritual power behind them. Jesus said, …*"The words I speak to you, they are spirit and they are life"* (John 6:63 NKJV).

The Word of God is the most powerful thing in the universe; through it Jesus made the universe. God's Word is an active force; creating, animating, sustaining, and propelling all things according to God's will.

In Matthew 24:35 it says, *"Heaven and earth will pass away, but My words will by no means ever pass away"* (NKJV). Because the Word is such a cosmic power, we can be sure ALL God's promises to us will be answered when we claim them. They cannot return void.

6) GOD IS FOR YOU

You are one of God's kids. God's love for you is unstoppable. In Scripture it says, *"What shall we say about such wonderful things as these? If God is for us, who can ever be against us?"* (Romans 8:31)

In the Message Bible, Romans 8:31-39 reads, *"So, what do you think? With God on our side like this, how can we lose? If God didn't hesitate to put everything on the line for us, embracing our condition and exposing himself to the worst by sending his own Son, is there anything else he wouldn't gladly and freely do for us? And who would dare tangle with God by messing with one of God's chosen? Who would dare even to point a finger? The One who died for us—who was raised to life for us!—is in the presence of God at this very moment sticking up for us. Do you think anyone is going to be able to drive a wedge between us and Christ's love for us? There is no way! Not trouble, not hard times, not hatred, not hunger, not homelessness, not bullying threats, not backstabbing, not even the worst sins listed in Scripture:*

They kill us in cold blood because they hate you. We're sitting ducks; they pick us off one by one. None of this fazes us because Jesus loves us. I'm absolutely convinced that nothing—nothing living or dead, angelic or demonic, today or tomorrow, high or low, thinkable or unthinkable—absolutely nothing can get between us and God's love because of the way that Jesus our Master has embraced us."

Because of this, we should be convinced that God will not withhold His help or love for us whenever we cry out to Him for help. God is faithful to those who are faithful to Him.

In conclusion, in Tony Evan's book of Illustrations, he tells a story that happened back in 2003.[1] A well-known minister and his wife were in New York. They checked out of their hotel and went to the airport to catch a flight back to Dallas. Once at the airport, they noticed it was shut down due to a power grid failure across the eastern seaboard. The minister got another hotel room near the airport, but it did not have electrical power, food, or hot water. All they had was candles, hot air, and a sweaty bed.

He looked out the window and saw the Marriott hotel a block away completely lit up with lights, music, laughter, food and drinks. All the rest of the city was dark. He walked over and asked the assistant manager, "Why is the rest of the city dark and yet you are lit up like a Christmas tree?"

The manager said, "It is very simple. When we built this hotel, we built it with a large gas generator in the basement. We have power on the inside that is not determined by circumstances on the outside. Even if there is nothing happening out there, there is plenty happening in here."

When you accepted Jesus Christ, He came to live in you on the inside. So what is happening on the outside should not determine whether or not you have a lighthouse on the inside. What happens outside should not determine your joy.

God has given you a power in your soul through your relationship with Jesus Christ. We don't have to live our lives as derived from life's circumstances.

Today, you may feel like God's plan for your life has gotten messed up. Are you ready to accept his new plan for your life? You have a destiny. Claim it. You have been bought with a price (the blood of Jesus). Greater is He that is in you than he that is in the world. You are a winner. Today is the day to take back what the enemy has stolen.

Four things to take charge of in your life:

1. Get on the right path with God.
2. Trust His plans for your life.
3. Do not be deceived by the devil's schemes.
4. Claim God's promises.

If you are a Christian, God is on your side and is fighting for you. Let's stay filled with the Holy Spirit and then the world will not impact us as much.

If you are ready to give your life over to Jesus Christ, simple say this prayer: "Father, I come to you in the name of Jesus. Forgive me for my sins and falling short of your glory. Come into my heart and make me a new creation in you. Fill me with your Holy Spirt and show me my purpose in you." Amen

♡ **Michael Hocker:** *When I was asked if I could write something reflecting on some memories of your ministry at our church, my mind started racing with all the thoughts and memories that would take up an entire book. What can I say in a "nutshell" that would summarize our two decades of relationship and do it justice? I will fight my well-known natural tendency to ramble and blither and take two hours to express what can be done in five minutes. No joke, am I right?*

It has been over twenty years of joyful experiences together, ranging from street bike rides to board Christmas parties and games to discipleship breakfasts at McDonalds every week during the younger time in my life. You were there for my baby dedications and water baptisms for my children, who are now entering adulthood. You were there as we served in ministry together, side by side, as you trusted me with the flock that you shepherd every Sunday morning as we lead them into worship and praise to our God.

Then there are the "real life" experiences together, which were more character-building times through trials and the tougher work of ministry. There were times of crying and praying over friends and family through rough times. There were times of crying and praying over each other over rough and trying times in our own lives. There were many years of monthly board meetings sitting around a meeting table with you to talk and pray through business, people, and building issues.

All this is to say that when I have been so blessed to spend so much time through the years with both of you through thick and thin, it allows us to honestly know each other deeply. It is not just how we work together through ministry and business but also how we get to know the true character of all its strengths and weaknesses. I have truly been blessed and honored to get to know both of you at this level because I can honestly say that through all of life's circumstances and how you have filled our pulpit and this pastor's office, you have done so with hearts full of love for God and the people of this church first and foremost. You have served with transparency and accountability, which are increasingly precious, rare, and priceless treasures these days.

How I deeply love and respect both of you and how I admire the Godly lives you demonstrate for everyone to observe and follow is what I can only hope and pray that people will say about me when I retire from my career. I always have, and I always will hold it dear to my heart all the times you have told me, "I have always considered you like one of my own children." The only way this sinks so deep for me is because of how much I respect and love both of you. My deep desire is that after you officially retire from our pulpit, I can take advantage of all that "extra free time" you have in your retired life to spend more time hanging out with you, creating more memories and times of fellowship. I love you both!

With tons of love, respect, and gratitude, Mike Hocker

PS. My apologies: I was asked to write a paragraph, and well....you know me. Whoops.

CHAPTER 14

Cultivating Thankfulness

TODAY, WE ARE GOING TO talk about cultivating an attitude of thankfulness. To illustrate this talk, I will tell you a short story:

One day, a woman was rushing home from a doctor's appointment. The doctor had been late, so by the time she left the clinic, she was running quite a bit behind schedule. She still had to pick up her prescription, pick up the children from the babysitter, and get home and make dinner.

As she began to circle the busy store parking lot, looking for a space, the heavens opened up with one of those massive downpours. While she usually wasn't one to bother God with the small stuff, she began to pray as she turned down the row closest to the front door. "Lord, you know what kind of a day I've had, and there's still so much to do. Could you please get me a close-in parking space so I don't get soaked?"

The words weren't even entirely out of her mouth when she saw a car's backup lights come on at the end of the row. It was the best space in the parking lot, straight out from the front door. She headed straight for it, and as she pulled in, she said, "Never mind God, something just opened up."

How many times do we pass up saying a simple "thank you" to the one who gives every good thing we have? That is certainly the case as we look today at Luke 17:11-19:

11As Jesus continued on toward Jerusalem, he reached the border between Galilee and Samaria. As he entered a village there, ten men with leprosy stood at a distance, crying out, "Jesus, Master, have mercy on us!" He looked at them and said, "Go show yourselves to the priests. And as they went, they were cleansed of their leprosy.

[15] One of them, when he saw that he was healed, came back to Jesus, shouting, "Praise God!" He fell to the ground at Jesus' feet, thanking him for what he had done. This man was a Samaritan. Jesus asked, "Didn't I heal ten men? Where are the other nine? Has no one returned to give glory to God except this foreigner?" And Jesus said to the man, "Stand up and go. Your faith has healed you."

Ten lepers! Ten men were desperate for a miracle, and only one of the ten came back to say thank you. In Biblical times, the word "leprosy" was used to describe all kinds of skin diseases, and the prognosis was tough: you were potentially contagious and cut off from the community. You could no longer live at home with your family, shop with others at the market, or sit with friends in the Synagogue. You had to keep your face covered and live separately with other lepers, never mingling with the clean people.

You had to announce, "Unclean!" and stay away from the crowds everywhere you went.

And everyone suspected that your disease was some divine judgment for your sin. So, leprosy was a social and spiritual ailment as much as a physical one—no wonders these ten lepers cried out for mercy.

William Barclay said, "Here is an example of a great law of life. A common misfortune has broken down the racial and national barriers. In the everyday tragedy of their leprosy, they had forgotten they were Jews and Samaritans and only remembered they were men in need."[1]

Isn't that what always levels the playing field when we discover and admit we are all just people in need?

There is no story in all the gospels so poignantly showing man's ingratitude!

These lepers came to Jesus in desperate need. He cured them, and nine never came back to say thank you! It's sad but true that once people get what they want, they never return! They had to cry out because they couldn't get too close to Jesus. And they needed mercy because most of these skin diseases had no known cure.

The term "mercy" means "not getting what you deserve." They probably felt condemned by God and were hurting all over. They had probably heard the news about Jesus, so when they saw him coming their way, they appealed to Jesus to bring some kind of relief.

And relief he brought. As it was written in the Law of Moses, Jesus told them to go to the priest and be declared clean. The priests functioned as health inspectors back then. Scripture says, "As they were going," the lepers were healed.

Interestingly, Jesus called them to take a step of faith in their healing. He didn't just heal them first and then send them on their way. He told the lepers to go ahead as if they had already been healed. And as they obeyed and stepped out on faith, they experienced a miracle of God at work.

Can you imagine how astonished these ten men must have been as they started their walk to the Synagogue and began to see the leprosy vanish from their skin? The white spots began to disappear, and life as they once knew it began to return. They must have been completely blown away!

At first, they may have had doubts. Still, as soon as Jesus healed them, they probably began planning big family reunions and beautiful celebrations that night. No doubt, they had much on their minds. It might seem almost excusable that they forgot to return and thank Jesus for what he had done for them.

But one of them remembered. As soon as the one man noticed his healing, he stopped his re-entry into society and returned to the source. He paused in his busy schedule and acknowledged his great gift by thanking the great giver.

And using that same loud voice of before, he fell at Jesus' feet and worshiped God. He got it right.

Jesus noticed that this thankful leper was a Samaritan, a half-Jew, the least likely to appreciate a miracle from the hand of a Jewish man. Yet, he did appreciate it, and he was rewarded for it. Jesus told him, "Go in peace. Your faith has made you whole."

I think the point is pretty simple today: You and I need to cultivate an ongoing "attitude of thankfulness" in our lives.

We need to be thankful for the little things: waking up in the morning, the sunrise, the sunsets, the stars at night, noticing the people around us, giving and receiving a smile, tasting a bite of a delicious Big Mac, watching yours or someone else's grandchild playing, feeling alive (even when it hurts).

I have shared with you before that we need to walk slower through the crowd to notice the need around us and be thankful to those who bless our lives.

Thank you, Father. Thank you, Jesus. Thank you, Holy Spirit. You are good and gracious, kind and merciful, loving, caring, compassionate, tender, and forgiving toward all of us!

Scripture says in James 1:17, "*Whatever is good and perfect is a gift coming down to us from God our Father, who created all the lights in the heavens…*," So I want to say, 'Thank you.'"

We all know what it feels like when someone genuinely thanks you. And you know how it feels when a person doesn't after you have bent over backward to serve someone and seem like they don't even appreciate it. I wonder how many times God feels that way about us.

Some of you may be thinking, "I'd be more thankful if life didn't hurt so much. There are too many things not to be thankful for!" In that case, you need to cultivate an attitude of thankfulness most of all! Being thankful is good for your health.

In 2015 Robert Emmons, professor of psychology at the University of California in Davis,[2] says, "Clinical trials indicate that the practice of gratitude can have dramatic and lasting effects in a person's life: It can lower blood pressure, improve immune function and facilitate more efficient sleep." They also linked gratefulness with better heart health, specifically less inflammation and healthier heart rhythms. Paul Mills, another researcher, found that thankful people "showed a better well-being, a less depressed mood, and less fatigue, resulting in better sleep." Optimism links to people having more disease-fighting cells in their bodies.

And if that's not enough, consider this: People who keep a gratitude journal have a reduced dietary fat intake – as much as 25 percent lower. Stress hormones like cortisol are 23 percent lower in grateful people. And having a daily gratitude practice could reduce the effects of aging on the brain.[3]

Science merely documents the goodness of obeying God, who says in his Word, "Be *thankful in all circumstances; for this is God's will for you who belong to Christ Jesus*" (1 Thessalonians 5:18).

We often ask how I can be thankful for everything. How can I be grateful for my life's terrible trials and crises? But, let me remind you, the Word says "**in**" all things, not "**for**" all things. There is a difference. I believe God means that we thank Him for His presence, power, and help as we walk through the trials and crises in our lives. Do you want to know God's will for you? It's to cultivate an attitude of thankfulness.

I talked about being thankful for the little things, but what about the big stuff? For these lepers, being restored physically and socially was huge. To return to health, to their families, not to be an outcast, avoided and probably ridiculed for years.

And what about the greatest gift of all: God himself? The fact that we can call God our Father, that we can be adopted into his family and have all our sins forgiven, that we can call Jesus our savior, our friend, that we never have to be alone again, even in the valley of the shadow of death, that "*he who is in you is greater than he who is in the world*"(1 John 4:4 NKJV).

Do we ever thank God for our salvation, for saving us from our sins and ourselves? Jesus said to the last leper, "Rise and go; your faith has made you whole." The most literal translation of what Jesus told him is, "Your faith has saved you." This leper found salvation both physically and spiritually.

God, we thank you for giving all of us the faith to lead us to salvation.

♡ **Jennifer Allen:** *Pastor Duane and Gretchen: I am so sorry to see you two retire. I tell everyone I came to the church the month after Pastor Duane decided to join the Redmond Assembly of God. I have grown a lot since starting Celebrate Recovery. I know you have seen this in me. I wish you the best in your retirement season. Hugs, Jennifer Allen*

♡ **Sharon Howells:** *I met Pastor Duane at a CR (Celebrate Recovery) car wash in July 2017. I had recently started to attend the Redmond Assembly during Pastor's vacation. At the next worship service during the fellowship, I shook hands with Pastor, and he remembered my name! I was amazed! He is so kind and personable! I met Gretchen shortly after that. She is genuinely interested in others and* *asks me how my family is doing nearly every time I see her. I took several classes at Bible Study taught by Gretchen. A memorable class was "The Bait of Satan." That class changed how I view issues in my life: the importance of forgiveness and not taking offense at others' behaviors. I have been attending the Redmond Assembly as a member for nearly seven years. To me, Pastor Duane and Gretchen are friends whom I love dearly. I wish both of them well in retirement. I will miss them! Sharon Howells*

CHAPTER 15

Easter – Life Changing

WHAT A WONDERFUL DAY! WE are celebrating Easter, the resurrection of Jesus Christ! Jesus Christ's resurrection is the greatest event of all time. It is the most powerful event in human history. The reason I say this is because it is the resurrection of Jesus that has changed the direction and the course of all of our lives.

In our society, some people will say, "So what?" What difference does Easter make and how does it apply to me? So, what if Jesus is alive? What's the big deal? How can something that happened over 2000 years ago have anything to do with my life today?

This was the same basic question they were asking in the city of Corinth back in the Apostle Paul's day, and it's something that needs to be answered in our day as well. Just how important is the resurrection? Let's read 1 Corinthians 15:12-20:

"But tell me this—since we preach that Christ rose from the dead, why are some of you saying there will be no resurrection of the dead? For if there is no resurrection of the dead, then Christ has not been raised either. And if Christ has not been raised, then all our preaching is useless, and your faith is useless. And we apostles would all be lying about God—for we have said that God raised Christ from the grave. But that can't be true if there is no resurrection of the dead. And if there is no resurrection of the dead, then Christ has not been raised. And if Christ has not been raised, then your faith is useless and you are still guilty of your sins. In that case, all who have died believing in Christ are lost! And if our hope in Christ is only for this life, we are more to be pitied than anyone in the world. But

in fact, Christ has been raised from the dead. He is the first of a great harvest of all who have died."

So Paul begins by telling them that Jesus's resurrection is what holds the whole basis of our faith together. If Jesus didn't rise from the dead, then all that we believe and hold onto, is empty and useless.

If Jesus didn't rise from the dead then Paul and all the other believers were nothing but liars, and all humanity remains condemned because of sin, and all those who have died have done so in their sin and are eternally lost.

But he doesn't stop there; Paul is saying that if Jesus didn't rise from the dead, then all those who believe should be pitied, because their whole life and belief structure is a complete waste of time.

But the good news is that Paul doesn't leave them or us hanging there. Verse 20 tells us, "But *in fact, Christ has been raised from the dead. He is the first of a great harvest of all who have die"* (1 Corinthians 15:20).

The resurrection is a proven historical fact, and it is a matter of public record. And yet, a very high percentage of people who say they believe in the resurrection don't live out their faith on a daily basis. I think it might be because they just don't get it, they don't get 'why' it is that important.

So what difference does Easter make? What difference does the resurrection make? Because of Easter, Jesus rose from the dead.

OUR SINS ARE FORGIVEN

I don't think there's a person alive that doesn't want a do-over in life. You know, where they can have a brand-new start in order to right all the mistakes they made.

All our failures, our problems, the bad decisions, our mistakes; along with all the stuff that has tortured us with painful memories, and believe we have to pay for the rest of our lives;

The resurrection of Jesus Christ is about having all of these things forgiven and done away with forever.

In Colossians 2:13-15 it tells us, *"You were dead because of your sins and because your sinful nature was not yet cut away. Then God made you alive with*

Christ, for he forgave all our sins. He canceled the record of the charges against us and took it away by nailing it to the cross. In this way, he disarmed the spiritual rulers and authorities. He shamed them publicly by his victory over them on the cross".

Jesus has wiped them out, and taken them out of the way, nailing them to the cross. In other words, Jesus has forgiven you for all your sins. He has wiped out the shameful evidence of broken laws and commandments, which has always hung over our heads. Jesus completely annulled it by nailing it over his own head on the cross.

Jesus paid the full penalty for our sins when He became that perfect sinless sacrifice upon the cross. And by His death He accomplished what God had planned from the very beginning saying, *"It is finished"*… (John 19:30).

What Jesus meant by those words is that His task, His work and God's purpose were completed and fulfilled. When we accept Jesus Christ into our hearts, asking Him to be our Savior and Lord, we can have the same assurance of Apostle Paul.

"There is therefore now no condemnation to those who are in Christ Jesus, who do not walk according to the flesh, but according to the Spirit" (Romans 8:1NKJV).

Now let us talk about the second difference Easter makes.

OUR LIVES HAVE PURPOSE

What was the Father's purpose for Jesus's death?

Jesus says in John 12:47,…*"I did not come to judge the world but to save the world" (NKJV).*

Paul said, *"But God demonstrates His own love toward us, in that while we were still sinners, Christ died for us"* (Romans 5:8 NKJV).

And again, Paul said, *"If you confess with your mouth the Lord Jesus and believe in your heart that God has raised Him from the dead, you will be saved"* (Romans 10:9_NKJV).

It was the Father's purpose to send Jesus so that through His death He would save all who would believe in Him. Because Jesus rose from the dead;

my faith, your faith is not empty or useless, but alive and vital for eternal life. Because of Jesus's death and resurrection, just as He promised, we can have an abundant life right now.

"*...I have come that they may have life, and that they may have it more abundantly*" (John 10:10 NKJV).

Jesus came not only to forgive our sin and give us eternal life, which is more than any of us deserve, but He also wants to give us abundant life right now. He wants to give us a life full of meaning and purpose.

But this isn't what society is trying to sell us. Society says that unless we have attained a certain social status, or acquired certain material possessions, we'll never be happy and productive.

I mean, how did we ever get along without Siri and Alexa? How can we survive without the latest smart TV, smart phone, tablet, and computer? The reality is that most people aren't really living, instead they merely exist. They get up in the morning, go to work, come home, eat dinner, watch some TV, or play on their computer, and then go to bed, only to repeat this scenario day in and day out.

Others take the King Solomon's route, which is, finding their purpose through pleasure, prestige, and power. But what they don't see is that in the end Solomon found it all useless and a complete waste of time.

But God created us for a purpose. He has a plan for our lives even before we were born. "*For we are His workmanship, created in Christ Jesus for good works, which God prepared beforehand that we should walk in them*" (Ephesians 2:10 NKJV).

That word, "workmanship," or in other translations, "masterpiece," means a work of art. What is being said is that each of us is God's unique work of art.

God has a plan for our lives, one that He wants us to fulfill. The tragedy is that few have discovered it. But as we continue to grow together in the Lord we'll learn of God's unique design.

Acts 20:24 states, "*But life is worth nothing unless I use it for doing the work assigned me by the Lord Jesus—the work of telling others the Good News about God's mighty kindness and love.*"

You see, while each of us have been uniquely designed by God, He has done so with His ultimate purpose in mind, and that is to bring the Good News to those He puts within our circle of influence.

The question then becomes how can we accomplish this?

THROUGH THE POWER OF CHRIST

Consider the power of Christ who said, "…*I lay down My life that I may take it again. No one takes it from Me, but I lay it down of Myself. I have power to lay it down, and I have power to take it again…*" (John 10:17-18 NKJV).

It was the resurrection that proved Jesus's power, the power over death and the grave. The religious leaders of that day, those who today we'd label as skeptics, mocked Jesus saying, "Hey, if you truly are the Son of God, come down off that cross." They wanted Jesus to display his power.

But Jesus was going to do something greater and more powerful than what they could even imagined. He was going to let the Romans kill Him, and place Him in the tomb, but in three days He was going to show them what true power is really all about as He came back to life proving who He claimed to be.

Now, the really cool part is that this same power that raised Jesus from the grave is available to us. "*I also pray that you will understand the incredible greatness of God's power for us who believe him. This is the same mighty power that raised Christ from the dead and seated him in the place of honor at God's right hand in the heavenly realms*" (Ephesians 1:19-20).

So, not only do we have a purpose for our lives, but Jesus has given to us His incredible power to live it out through belief in Him.

Jesus gives us the power to change what we cannot change on our own. Our hurts, our habits, and hang ups.

It is the power to let go of guilt, the grudges, and the grief that keeps us stuck in the past.

It is the power to forgive others that keeps us going when all we want to do is quit.

This is why we can say with Paul, "I can do everything through Christ who gives me strength" (Philippians 4:13).

Along with the power of Christ, we also have His promises to help us live according to God's purposes.

THROUGH THE PROMISES OF CHRIST

Some of these incredible promises are:

Jesus told him. "I am the way, the truth, and the life. No one comes to the Father except through Me" (John 14:6).

"Yes, ask me for anything in My name, and I will do it" (John 14:14).

"Behold, we are going up to Jerusalem, and the Son of Man will be betrayed to the chief priests and to the scribes; and they will condemn Him to death, and deliver Him to the Gentiles to mock and to scourge and to crucify. And the third day He will rise again" (Matthew 20:18-19 NKJV).

Easter proves that God keeps His promises, which is what Moses and the Apostle Paul tells us. Moses *"God is not human, that he should lie, not a human being, that he should change his mind. Does he speak and then not act? Does he promise and not fulfill"* (Numbers 23:19 NIV)?

Apostle Paul says in 2 Corinthians 1:20, *"For all the promises of God in Him are 'Yes', and in Him Amen, to the glory of God through us (NKJV).*

Jesus makes this promise. *"I tell you the truth, those who listen to my message and believe in God who sent me have eternal life. They will never be condemned for their sins, but they have already passed from death into life"* (John 5:24).

Everyone is going to die, that's a given, because no one will live this life forever. Yet, as common and well understood as this fact is, no one really likes to discuss or talk about it, and that is because death scares us. But, literally millions of people go through life totally unprepared for something they know is certain to happen.

The writer of Hebrews 9:27 (paraphrase) says that everyone has been appointed a time to die and afterwards stand before God in judgment. So, here's the question, do you know where you'll spend eternity? And what do you base that decision upon? What promises?

This leads me to the last point, which is because of Jesus's resurrection.

Our Future is Secure

If we were to take a survey and ask people if they were sure they were going to heaven, the most common answer would be, "I hope so." But isn't that something we should want to be 100 percent sure of?

Most people base their answers on wrong information, wrong motives, and misunderstandings perpetrated by science, religion, and our materialistic culture.

Some believe in Salvation by Sincerity: It doesn't matter what you believe as long as you're sincere. I once read of a pilot who built his own airplane and sincerely thought it would fly. But He was sincerely wrong.

Others believe in Salvation through Good Works: People believe that their good works will get them into God's good graces and heaven. But the Bible says, *"For by grace you have been saved through faith, and that not of yourselves; it is the gift of God, not of works, lest anyone should boast"* (Ephesians 2:8-9 NKJV).

Then there is Salvation by being better: People believe they get to heaven by giving up stuff, like smoking, drinking, cussing, and a hundred other vices that people have. But the Bible says, *"There is a way that seems right to a man, but its end is the way of death"* (Proverbs 16:25 NKJV).

Some take the route of Salvation by Ritual: People join a church, say certain kinds of prayers, and perform certain rituals. Sitting in a church doesn't make a person a Christian any more than putting kittens in your oven makes them biscuits.

Then there is Salvation by Heritage: People say they are a Christian because their parents are Christians. But John the Baptist confronts this sort of teaching saying, *"Don't just say to each other, 'We're safe, for we are descendants of Abraham.' That means nothing, for I tell you, God can create children of Abraham from these very stones"* (Matthew 3:9).

And finally, there are those who believe in Salvation by comparing themselves to someone else: People say, "At least I am not like that person" or "At least I haven't_____ and you can fill in your own blank here." The Bible says, *"Oh, don't worry; we wouldn't dare say that we are as wonderful as these other men who tell you how important they are! But they are only comparing themselves with each other, using themselves as the standard of measurement. How ignorant"* (2 Corinthians 10:12)!

Salvation and eternal life with God comes only through having a personal relationship with Jesus Christ. In John 17:3 it wisely says, *"And this is eternal life, that they may know You, the only true God, and Jesus Christ whom You have sent"* (NKJV).

"All praise to God, the Father of our Lord Jesus Christ. It is by his great mercy that we have been born again, because God raised Jesus Christ from the dead..." (1 Peter 1:3).

What we could say is that Salvation isn't about "what" we know; rather it's about "who" we know. And the "who" we know should be Jesus.

One day we're all going to stand before God and He will ask, "Why should I let you into My heaven?" Now we could answer, "Well I was sincere in my beliefs, I did a lot of good things, I didn't cuss, drink, smoke, or chew or go with any girls that do. I went to church and even got baptized, and since my parents are Christians don't I get a free pass?"

And God will say, "I'm sorry." Or we could say, "I'm Your Son Jesus's, newest friend. I accepted Him as my Savior and Lord." And God will say... *"Well done, good and faithful servant...enter into the joy of your Lord"* (Matthew 25:21NKJV).

What difference does Easter make? Because Jesus died and rose from the dead, our sins are forgiven, we have a purpose to live out through the power and promises of Christ, and our eternal future is secured in heaven.

Easter's message is a life changing message. That we can have a brand new life and an eternity with God, and that's because all of God's promises are true.

♡ **Roger & Donna Brown**: *Congratulations, Duane and Gretchen on your retirement. We have been blessed to have you as our pastor for twenty-one years. It took perseverance and a miracle to carry on all these years since your diagnosis and we continue to pray for healing. We hope you enjoy your next journey in life with six Saturdays and one Sunday every week. We love you both. Roger & Donna*

♡ **Darlene Shackelford**: *Congratulations on your well-deserved retirement. Thank you so much for your prayers and visits when Bob was in hospice care at Regency. I will miss your great sermons and funny stories. I hope and pray you both have a great retirement on your Terrebonne farm. Since we are neighbors, please feel free to stop by any time. Love you both. Darlene Shackelford*

CHAPTER 16
Understanding Communion

COMMUNION, WHICH IS OFTEN TIMES called the Lord's Supper, was instituted by Jesus Christ on the night of His betrayal while celebrating the Passover with His twelve disciples. As God had done in the past, He was giving them a "truth" to act upon time and time again. He used the unleavened bread and the cup (wine or grape juice) to portray a fundamental truth of our salvation. Jesus said some very profound and startling things. For instance: He said the bread was His body and the wine was His blood and that He was sealing a New Covenant with them with the drinking of the cup.

In Matthew 26:17-30 we read, *"On the first day of the Feast of Unleavened Bread, the disciples came to Jesus and asked, "Where do you want us to make preparations for you to eat the Passover?"* [18] *He replied, "Go into the city to a certain man and tell him, 'The Teacher says: My appointed time is near. I am going to celebrate the Passover with my disciples at your house.'"* [19] *So the disciples did as Jesus had directed them and prepared the Passover.* [20] *When evening came, Jesus was reclining at the table with the Twelve.* [21] *And while they were eating, he said, "I tell you the truth, one of you will betray me."* [22] *They were very sad and began to say to him one after the other, "Surely you don't mean me, Lord?"*

[23] *Jesus replied, "The one who has dipped his hand into the bowl with me will betray me.* [24] *The Son of Man will go just as it is written about him. But woe to that man who betrays the Son of Man! It would be better for him if he had not been born."* [25] *Then Judas, the one who would betray him, said, "Surely you don't mean me, Rabbi?" Jesus answered, "Yes, you have said so."* [26] *While they were eating, Jesus took bread, gave thanks and broke it, and gave it to his disciples, saying,*

"Take and eat; this is my body." [27]*Then he took the cup, gave thanks and offered it to them, saying, "Drink from it, all of you.* [28]*This is my blood of the covenant, which is poured out for many for the forgiveness of sins.* [29]*I tell you, I will not drink of this fruit of the vine from now on until that day when I drink it anew with you in my Father's kingdom."* [30]*When they had sung a hymn, they went out to the Mount of Olives"* (NIV).

The Old Covenant (Old Testament) was based on blood sacrifice of animals. For thousands of years, the innocent animal was brought before the priest, the person confessed their sin, then the person killed the animal, and the priest offered the blood as a sacrifice in that persons place.

Leviticus 1:1-4 states, *"The LORD called to Moses and spoke to him from the tent of meeting. He said, "Speak to the Israelites and say to them: 'When anyone among you brings an offering to the LORD, bring as your offering an animal from either the herd or the flock. If the offering is a burnt offering from the herd, you are to offer a male without defect. You must present it at the entrance to the tent of meeting so that it will be acceptable to the LORD. You are to lay your hand on the head of the burnt offering, and it will be accepted on your behalf to make atonement for you"* (NIV).

In the New Testament when John the Baptist was making reference to Jesus, he said to his followers in John 1:29, ...*"Look the Lamb of God, who takes away the sin of world"*(NIV). John the Baptist was making a direct correlation to the Old Testament sin offering.

For thousands of years the people of God acted out the redemptive story and the truth that forgiveness of sin required a blood sacrifice. Now, the Lamb of God, Jesus Christ Himself, arrived at the appointed time in history to make that sacrifice once and for all.

So now for over two thousand years, Christians have continued to act out by keeping alive the sacred memory of what Jesus Christ did on the Cross. As the body of Christ or believers we are drawn together and in common partake in essence of Christ in a "memorial service".

In 1 Corinthians 11:23-31 we read as the Apostle Paul instructs the Corinthian church; [23]*"For I received from the Lord what I also passed on to you: The Lord Jesus, on the night he was betrayed, took bread,* [24]*and when he had given*

thanks, he broke it and said, "This is my body, which is for you; do this in remem-
*brance of me." *[25]* In the same way, after supper he took the cup, saying, "This cup*
is the new covenant in my blood; do this, whenever you drink it, in remembrance
*of me." *[26]* For whenever you eat this bread and drink this cup, you proclaim the*
*Lord's death until he comes. *[27]* Therefore, whoever eats the bread or drinks the cup*
of the Lord in an unworthy manner will be guilty of sinning against the body and
*blood of the Lord. *[28]* A man ought to examine himself before he eats of the bread*
*and drinks of the cup. *[29]* For anyone who eats and drinks without discerning the*
*body of the Lord eats and drinks judgment on himself. *[30]* That is why many among*
you are weak and sick, and a number of you have fallen asleep," But if we were
more discerning with regard to ourselves, we would not come under such judgment
"(NIV).

We will notice in this passage in verse 27 and 28; "*Therefore, whoever eats*
the bread or drinks the cup of the Lord in an unworthy manner will be guilty of
sinning against the body and blood of the Lord. A man ought to examine himself
before he eats of the bread and drinks of the cup" (NIV).

What the Apostle Paul was saying is that the church had begun to practice
communion as a ritual. Just something they did without thought or meaning
or feeling. We notice that Paul said that it was not the failure of discerning the
blood, but a failure to discern the body that caused the people to be weak and
sick, and to die before their time.

We must not find ourselves combining these two elements of communion
together. There is a two-fold application which these two elements represent.

1. THE BLOOD FOR FORGIVENESS

The Corinthians like most Christians today, had no problem discerning the blood. Paul's epistle makes it very clear that the blood of Jesus
brings forgiveness of sins. Colossians 1:13-14 reads; "*For he has rescued*
us from the dominion of darkness and brought us into the kingdom of
the Son he loves, in whom we have redemption, the forgiveness of sins"
(NIV).

Ephesians 1:7 reads; *"In him we have redemption through his blood, the forgiveness of sins, in accordance with the riches of God's grace"* (NIV).

Because the Son of God paid the penalty for our sins with His spotless blood, we can go free when we put our trust in His blood to save us. When you partake of the cup, we remember that we have been forgiven and have been made righteous. The blood of Jesus has given you right standing before God, so that you can come boldly into His presence. When you pray, you can be sure He hears you!

2. THE BREAD FOR HEALING

In the Scripture the prophet Isaiah 53:4-6 said; *"Yet it was our weaknesses he carried; it was our sorrows that weighed him down. And we thought his troubles were a punishment from God for his own sins! But he was wounded and crushed for our sins. He was beaten that we might have peace. He was whipped, and we were healed! All of us have strayed away like sheep. We have left God's paths to follow our own. Yet the LORD laid on him the guilt and sins of us all.*

The Young's Literal Translation Bible uses the words "grief" and "sorrows" stating that *"surely our sickness He hath borne, and our pains He hath carried them…* The same way in the Gospel of Matthew 8:17 where it states *"He himself took our infirmities and bore our sickness."*

In the Greek, "infirmities" or ostheneia means bodily weakness. So as Isaiah ways saying; the Messiah would take upon His own body, our bodily weaknesses, sicknesses, and pains. In other words, Jesus bore not just our sins, but also our bodily weaknesses, sicknesses and pains.

David also described what the Lord did for us in Psalm 103:2-3 when he said; *"Praise the LORD, O my soul, and forget not all his benefits*

—who forgives all your sins and heals all your diseases, who redeems your life from the pit and crowns you with love and compassion" (NIV).

You see, His benefits include the forgiveness of our sins and the healing of our diseases. When Jesus took our punishment on the cross, it did not just bring us forgiveness; it also brought us healing.

If you ask most Christians whether they are sure of their forgiveness, they will say yes. They will tell you that God forgives them because of what Jesus did on the cross. But if you ask them if they are sure about their healing, they might say I'm not sure.

Let me share a profound truth from God's Word: Jesus bore our sins and sickness on the cross according to God's Word. So our healing, like forgiveness, is not just a promise; it is blood-bought right for the child of God. Because of what Jesus did on the cross, we have forgiveness and healing or wholeness; they go hand in hand.

Your faith in Christ for forgiveness is the same faith that will bring you healing.

When you hold the bread in your hand, you are coming in touch with the greatest expression of His love. This bread is the love that made Jesus endure the cruel stripes on his back and caused him to subject his body to be beaten, bruised, and broken so your body and my body can be whole.

When we share communion, you celebrate and release our faith to receive His health and wholeness in exchange for your sickness and disease. When we drink the cup, we are reminded that the blood of the sinless Son of God did not just bring you forgiveness but made you forever righteous, blameless, and holy. Because of this, we have perfect standing before the Father.

So, to rightly discern it, acknowledge and know the purpose of what Christ did for you on the cross. Remember, and do not view this act as some religious form, a religious rite or ritual, but remember the great price Jesus paid for our forgiveness and our healing.

For over two thousand years, Christians have continued to act out what we might call a "living sermon" by keeping alive the sacred memory of Jesus' supreme love on the cross. Believers worldwide, as the Body of Christ, are drawn together and partake of the essence of Christ in this memorial service. I want to look at five proclamations of this wonderful commemoration that salvation is solely through the broken body and shed blood of Jesus Christ.

Proclamations of Communion - A proclamation is an official declaration issued by a person to make a certain announcement know.

1. **Our participation in the redemption of Jesus Christ**

   I've been redeemed. Jesus paid the price for me.

   In Matthew 26:26-29 "While they were eating, Jesus took some bread, and after a blessing, He broke it and gave it to the disciples, and said, *"Take, eat; this is my body." And when He had taken a cup and given thanks, He gave it to them, saying, "Drink from it, all of you. This is my blood of the covenant, which is poured out for many for forgiveness of sins. "I tell you, I will not drink of this fruit of the vine from now on until that day when I drink it anew with you in my Father's kingdom""*(NIV).

2. **Our participation in the life of Jesus Christ**

   Luke 22:14-20 reads, *"[14]When the time came, Jesus and the apostles sat down together at the table.[15]Jesus said, "I have been very eager to eat this Passover meal with you before my suffering begins. [16]For I tell you now that I won't eat this meal again until its meaning is fulfilled in the Kingdom of God."*

   [17]Then he took a cup of wine and gave thanks to God for it. Then he said, "Take this and share it among yourselves. [18]For I will not drink wine again until the Kingdom of God has come."

¹⁹He took some bread and gave thanks to God for it. Then he broke it in pieces and gave it to the disciples, saying, "This is my body, which is given for you. Do this in remembrance of me."

²⁰After supper he took another cup of wine and said, "This cup is the new covenant between God and his people—an agreement confirmed with my blood, which is poured out as a sacrifice for you".

3. Our participation in the family of God

1 Corinthians 10:16-17 states, *"When we bless the cup at the Lord's Table, aren't we sharing in the benefits of the blood of Christ? And when we break the loaf of bread, aren't we sharing in the benefits of the body of Christ? And we all eat from one loaf, showing that we are one body."*

4. Our participation in the ministry of Jesus Christ

We read in 1 Corinthians 11:23-26, *"For I pass on to you what I received from the Lord himself. On the night when he was betrayed, the Lord Jesus took some bread and gave thanks to God for it. Then he broke it in pieces and said, "This is my body, which is given for you. Do this in remembrance of me." In the same way, he took the cup of wine after supper, saying, "This cup is the new covenant between God and his people—an agreement confirmed with my blood. Do this in remembrance of me as often as you drink it." For every time you eat this bread and drink this cup, you are announcing the Lord's death until he comes again".*

5. Our participation in the unity of the Body of Christ

The Bible reads in Ephesians 4:3-6, *"Make every effort to keep the unity of the Spirit through the bond of peace. There is one body and one Spirit, just as you were called to one hope when you were called; one Lord, one faith, one baptism; one God and Father of all, who is over all and through all and in all"* (NIV).

Again, before you receive, remember that the Holy Communion is not a ritual to be observed, but a blessing to be received. His loving instruction is that we are to remember Him as we partake of the Holy Communion. Jesus wanted us conscious of how His body was broken for our wholeness, and His blood was shed for the forgiveness of our sins. And whenever we partake in this consciousness, we "proclaim the Lord's death till He comes".

So what does this all mean? It means you and I belong, to Christ and to each other. We are accountable to Christ and to each other. We are to mutually care for each other. We are to have a shared vision and shared values. We are to pray for each other.

♡ **David King:** *Thank you so much for being my Pastors and guide for the past twenty-two years. In the fifty plus years I have been part of Redmond Assembly of God, I consider you to be most loving and caring. I have always and will continue to pray for you daily. May God bless your both in your retirement until the time He says, "Well done good and faithful servants." I love you. David King*

♡ **Janet King:** *I have shared so many memories and experiences with you for twenty-two years. Wow. I have been blessed to know you as my Pastors and friends. Our church body has grown and prospered in so many ways during your ministry with us. Thank you for your faithfulness. Words cannot adequately express my love, gratitude and how much you will be missed. You have shown how much God loves us with your encouragement, sermons, stories, and reminders, just to name a few. My daily prayer, Duane and Gretchen, is that God blesses your well-deserved retirement. I know that you will be God's ministers and servants in whatever you do, that is just who you are. Love, Janet King*

CHAPTER 17

Mother's Day - Empowering with Encouragement

WE ARE HERE TO CELEBRATE Jesus and recognize and celebrate the ladies in our lives. As your Pastor, I want to say "Happy Mother's Day to all the moms here today. Thank you for your investment and encouragement into the lives of so many--children, grandchildren, and to those of you who are spiritual parents or grandparents. My mom died in 2018, and she taught my sister and me all about Jesus. The prayers of moms help the family in their belief in God, which is encouragement.

There is an old story about a preacher leaving a church. At his farewell dinner, he tried to encourage one of the members, "Don't be so sad. The next preacher will be better than me." She replied, "That is what they said last time, but it keeps getting worse."

Life can be very challenging most of the time. Listening to today's news is not encouraging, so Gretchen and I have decided to turn the news off in our home. We must slowdown in our lifestyles and allow the Holy Spirit to speak to our hearts as we help the people around us.

What do people need when they are struggling? They need encouragement! What do people need when they need to be challenged to do something that may seem out of their normal range of ability? Encouragement! We face many challenges at every turn, and it is essential to have people who will get behind us and tell us we can do it.

I remember when my son, Colby, was four years old, and I wanted to teach him how to ride a bicycle. Colby looked at the training wheels and said, "What are those?" So, I took them off. As he pedaled the bike, I hung on to the back of the seat, and he said, "Daddy, don't let go, don't let go." Of course, as he pedaled faster, I couldn't keep up and had to let go. He crashed and got scratched up in the process and started crying. As he got up, I yelled, "Good job, Colby." I encouraged him even though he had crashed. He smiled through the tears and kept on trying. Even amid challenges, we need to continue to give encouragement.

William Arthur Ward said, "**Flatter me, and I may not believe you. Criticize me, and I may not like you. Ignore me, and I may not forgive you. Encourage me, and I will not forget you.**"[1]

Encouragement can genuinely change another person's life. Looking back at our lives, we can see all kinds of people who took the time to encourage us along the way.

WHAT IS ENCOURAGEMENT?

To encourage means to "come alongside." To 'encourage' others, we need to come alongside them and help them. It is not about telling them what they are doing wrong but encouraging them to stay the course.

The root for the word 'encourage' comes from the same word Jesus uses when speaking of the Holy Spirit in the following Scriptures:

John 14:16, 26, "*[16]And I will ask the Father, and He will give you another advocate to help you and be with you forever...[26]But the Advocate, the Holy Spirit, whom the Father will send in my name, will teach you all things and will remind you of everything I have said to you*" (NIV).

John 15:26, "*When the Advocate comes, whom I will send to you from the Father—the Spirit of truth who goes out from the Father—he will testify about me*" (NIV).

John 16:7, *"But very truly I tell you, it is for your good that I am going away. Unless I go away, the Advocate will not come to you; but if I go, I will send him to you"* (NIV).

An essential part of encouraging another person is the willingness to step in and walk beside them as an advocate. People will respond better to being admonished if they know you are willing to get into the trenches with them.

In Acts 4:36 (NIV) it states that Barnabas was a *"son of encouragement."* Barnabas was inspiring to be around, which must have been a good balance for the hard-charged Paul.

How Do We Encourage Others?

We get in the game with them.

In Acts 13, we see John Mark on the first missionary journey, but he turns back at Pamphylia. These missionary journeys were trips on which Paul would plant churches.

In Acts 15, it is time for the second missionary journey. Barnabas wants to take John Mark with them, but Paul is not going to participate in it.

If it were up to Paul, John Mark had his chance and failed.

Look at how Acts 15:36-39 records this event. *"Sometime later, Paul said to Barnabas, "Let us go back and visit the believers in all the towns where we preached the word of the Lord and see how they are doing." Barnabas wanted to take John, also called Mark, with them, but Paul did not think it wise to take him because he had deserted them in Pamphylia and had not continued with them in the work. They had such a sharp disagreement that they parted company. Barnabas took Mark and sailed for Cyprus"* (NIV).

John Mark could have been ruined for service to God if Barnabas had not been willing to take him along. Barnabas was willing to get into the game with John Mark.

We display a positive attitude

If we will encourage others, we must maintain a positive attitude. You can encourage someone while pushing them past what they think they can do if they see you have a positive attitude about them.

We instill faith in them

We must encourage or inspire faith in others. People will achieve great heights if they know someone believes in them. My mother helped instill faith in me by showing her faithfulness in church, home, work, and devotional life. I knew she prayed for me and loved me by how she instilled faith in me.

Why Do We Encourage Others

To keep those who are fainthearted from quitting.

1 Thessalonians 5:14 it states, *"And we urge you, brothers and sisters, warn those who are idle and disruptive, encourage the disheartened, help the weak, be patient with everyone"* (NIV).

To draw out the potential in them.

Remember John Mark, or "Mark" as we commonly know him, the writer of the second Gospel? Remember how Paul wanted nothing to do with him on the second missionary journey?

Look at **2 Timothy 4:11**, where it states**,** *"Only Luke is with me. Get Mark and bring him with you, because he is helpful to me in my ministry"*(NIV).

To help them see God in the tough times.

When the tough times of life hit us, we need to be encouraged that God is still in control. We need to know that God has a plan. This can be difficult to see when we are in the midst of the struggles of life. These two scriptures can help people through this:

James 1:2-4 *"Consider it pure joy, my brothers and sisters, whenever you face trials of many kinds, because you know that the testing of your faith produces perseverance. Let perseverance finish its work so that you may be mature and complete, not lacking anything" (NIV).*

Romans 8:28, *"And we know that in all things God works for the good of those who love him, who have been called according to his purpose"* (NIV).

To strengthen them.

We should always try to help strengthen others' faith. We need to make sure we are investing ourselves in other people in order to help them. I am personally in ministry to help strengthen others. Apostle Paul, when he was in prison, was always trying to encourage others.

In **Philippians 1:14**, Paul writes**,** *"And because of my chains, most of the brothers and sisters have become confident in the Lord and dare all the more to proclaim the gospel without fear"*(NIV).

Proverbs 27:17 – *"As iron sharpens iron, so one person sharpens another"* (NIV).

To strengthen the church community

We gather together on the first day of the week to help build one another up. We need each other, and a chain is only as strong as its weakest link. We must do all we can to strengthen the church family and the Christian community.

In **Hebrews 10:24-25** it states, *"Let us think of ways to motivate one another to acts of love and good works. And let us not neglect our meeting together, as some people do, but encourage one another, especially now that the day of his return is drawing near."*

In summary, encouragement is the ability to push one another in the right direction when needed. A little encouragement goes a long way. If you are an "I knew it would not work" or an "I told you so" person, it is time to get on the encouragement bandwagon.

We are called to be a blessing to others. Look for opportunities where you can bless someone with encouragement.

Moms and ladies, you are great encouragers and a gift to your children and grandchildren. Some of you may not feel like you are a good mom but know that we praise every mom in this room because you did the best you could with the knowledge you had. We are grateful, and so is God.

"She speaks with wisdom,
and faithful instruction is on her tongue".

— Proverbs 31:26 NIV

♡ **Dawn Smith:** *We moved here in 2012 and started attending Redmond Assembly of God. My husband Jonathan Smith had been a Sunday school teacher in our previous church and enjoyed teaching. He and Pastor Duane got along well and soon Jonathan was allowed to occasionally cover the class on Sunday* *nights. After a while he also occasionally covered for a Wednesday night. Then the opportunity came to teach a Sunday school class. He even hosted a video class on Creationism on a Sunday night. He only enjoyed six years of retirement before the Lord called him home, but I think his time of teaching and ministering at Redmond Assembly of God was the most enjoyable in his career. I thank the pastor for encouraging him to teach classes. Love Dawn*

CHAPTER 18

Father's Day Message

ON THIS SUNDAY MORNING, ON Father's Day, as I look across this room, I see a lot of men—good-looking, handsome, intelligent, hardworking, compassionate, caring men. Good men! Did you hear me? I said, "Good men"!

You are here this morning not out of obligation from your wives, but out of personal choice and commitment. Whether you are at the beginning of your journey with God, exploring Christianity, or have been serving the Lord for many years, your presence here is a testament to your personal desire and commitment.

You desire to be a better man, a better husband, a better father, and a better follower of Jesus, and I commend you and say thank you for who you are and your willingness to grow in your relationship with God and others.

Proverbs 4:1-13 gives good advice, *"My children, listen when your father corrects you. Pay attention and learn good judgment, ²for I am giving you good guidance. Don't turn away from my instructions. ³For I, too, was once my father's son, tenderly loved as my mother's only child. ⁴My father taught me, "Take my words to heart. Follow my commands, and you will live. ⁵Get wisdom; develop good judgment. Don't forget my words or turn away from them. ⁶Don't turn your back on wisdom, for she will protect you. Love her, and she will guard you. ⁷Getting wisdom is the wisest thing you can do! And whatever else you do, develop good judgment. ⁸If you prize wisdom, she will make you great. Embrace her, and she will honor you. ⁹She will place a lovely wreath on your head; she will present you with a beautiful crown."*

[10]*"My child, listen to me and do as I say, and you will have a long, good life.*[11]*I will teach you wisdom's ways and lead you in straight paths.*[12]*When you walk, you won't be held back; when you run, you won't stumble.*[13]*Take hold of my instructions; don't let them go. Guard them, for they are the key to life."*

I'd like to share four things from God's Word that I know, if you apply them to your life and practice them on a daily basis, you will grow in your relationship with God and with other people.

1. FIND A PLACE TO BE 'QUIET' OFTEN

Why is it that most people find silence and their own solitude very uncomfortable? It is not easy in this day and age to turn off the noise in our lives. We are constantly around other people. Music usually plays in the background of our cars and in the stores we shop in. To be alone and quiet without some activity going on in our lives is not easy. We usually want something to do to keep us busy and occupy our time, hands, and thoughts.

In his book *Dangers Men Face*, Jerry White said, "We desperately need time apart to give God space and time to work in our lives."[1]

After the beheading of John the Baptist in Mark 6, we see that after so many people were crowding around Jesus and His disciples, Jesus finally told the disciples in Mark 6:31, *"Then, because so many people were coming and going that they did not even have a chance to eat", he said to them, "Come with me by yourselves to a quiet place and get some rest"* (NIV)

Jesus understood he teaches each of them to take some time for solitude. His warning is simple "either come apart or fall apart."

What we know is this, to find time to be quiet is not a natural habit for any of us. Time apart has to be purposely scheduled. Jerry White says; we need to come away from the rush of our lives to think, reflect, pray, and recharge. How and when has to be determined by you, no one else can answer that question but you.[2]

How do we apply this to our lives? Start out with small steps. Maybe it's just turning off the radio on the drive to work to think, reflect, or to pray. Ask

God to help you shut off the noise in your life just for a few moments and give that time to Him.

2. GUARD YOUR HEART

As men we must be diligent to guard our hearts. King Solomon says it best in Proverbs 4:23, "Above all else, guard your heart, for it is the wellspring of life" (NIV). This is necessary for at least three reasons:

Because your heart is extremely valuable. We don't guard worthless things. I take my garbage to the street every Sunday night. It is picked up on Monday morning. It sits on the sidewalk all night, completely unguarded. Why? Because it is worthless.

Not so with your heart. It is the essence of who you are. It is your authentic self—the core of your being. It is where all your dreams, your desires, and your passions live. It is that part of you that connects with God and other people.

Just like your physical body, if your heart—your spiritual heart—dies, your leadership dies. This is why Solomon says, "Above all else." He doesn't say, "If you get around to it" or "It would be nice if." No, he says to make it your top priority.

Because your heart is the source of everything you do. King Solomon says it is the "wellspring of life." In other words, it is the source of everything else in your life. Your heart overflows into thoughts, words, and actions.

In Oregon, we have thousands and thousands of natural springs, where water flows to the surface of the earth from deep under the ground. It then accumulates in pools or runs off into creeks and streams.

If you plug up the spring, you stop the flow of water. If you poison the water, the flow becomes toxic. In either situation, you threaten life downstream. Everything depends on the condition of the spring.

Likewise, if your heart is unhealthy, it has an impact on everything else. It threatens your family, your friends, your ministry, your career, and, your legacy. It is imperative that you guard it.

Because your heart is under constant attack. When Solomon says to guard your heart, he implies that you are living in a combat zone—one in which there are casualties.

Many of us are unaware of the reality of this war. We have an enemy who is bent on our destruction. He not only opposes God, but he opposes everything that is aligned with God and His purposes-including us.

The enemy uses all kinds of weapons to attack our heart. For me, these attacks often come in the form of some circumstance that leads to disappointment, or discouragement, or even disillusionment. In these situations, I am tempted to quit—to walk off the field and surrender.

This is why if you and I are going to succeed as men—and survive as individuals—we must guard our hearts. They are more important than we can possibly imagine. If we lose heart, we have lost everything.

3. STUDY GOD'S WORD

In Psalms 86:11 it says, *"Teach me your ways, O LORD that I may live according to your truth! Grant me purity of heart, so that I may honor you."*

Psalm 25:4-5 reveals to us, "*Show me the right path, O LORD; point out the road for me to follow. Lead me by your truth and teach me, for you are the God who saves me. All day long I put my hope in you.*"

Reading the Bible shows us God's character. The Bible is our definitive source for the answers to our questions about God.

In the past God spoke to our ancestors through the prophets at many times and in various ways, but in these last days he has spoken to us by his Son, whom he appointed heir of all things, and through whom also he made the universe. The Son is the radiance of God's glory and the exact representation of his being, sustaining all things by his powerful word. After he had provided purification for sins, he sat down at the right hand of the Majesty in heaven" (Hebrews 1:1-3 NIV).

Reading the Bible teaches us to imitate God.
"*Follow God's example, therefore, as dearly loved children*" (Ephesians 5:1 NIV)

Reading the Bible helps us discover our next step.
"*Your word is a lamp for my feet, a light on my path*" (Psalms 119:105 NIV)

Reading the Bible keeps us from sin.
"*I have hidden your word in my heart that I might not sin against you*" (Psalm 119:11 NIV)

Reading the Bible helps us to renew our minds so we can know God's will.
"*Therefore, I urge you, brothers and sisters, in view of God's mercy, to offer your bodies as a living sacrifice, holy and pleasing to God—this is your true and proper worship. Do not conform to the pattern of this world, but be transformed by the renewing of your mind. Then you will be able to test and approve what God's will is—his good, pleasing and perfect will*" (Romans 12:1-2 NIV)

Reading the Bible allows us to be certain of what God said. The Bible is our final authority.

"Sanctify them by the truth; your word is truth" (John 17:17 NIV).

Reading the Bible allows us to receive the desires of our heart.

"If you remain in me and my words remain in you, ask whatever you wish, and it will be done for you" (John 15:7 NIV).

Reading the Bible is how we learn about the gospel.

"You study the Scriptures diligently because you think that in them you have eternal life. These are the very Scriptures that testify about me, yet you refuse to come to me to have life" (John 5:39-40 NIV)

Reading the Bible gives us courage.

"Keep this Book of the Law always on your lips; meditate on it day and night, so that you may be careful to do everything written in it. Then you will be prosperous and successful. Have I not commanded you? Be strong and courageous. Do not be afraid; do not be discouraged, for the Lord your God will be with you wherever you go" (Joshua 1:8-9 NIV).

Reading the Bible helps us to be fruitful.

"... but whose delight is in the law of the Lord, and who meditates on his law day and night. That person is like a tree planted by streams of water, which yields its fruit in season and whose leaf does not wither—whatever they do prospers" (Psalm 1:2-3 NIV).

Fellowship with Others.

We need each other. Guys listen. We can't be loners and expect to grow spiritually. There are a lot of men who think they don't need anybody. If that is the way a man feels it won't be long until that man begins to shut down emotionally and spiritually.

Proverbs 27:17,19 tells us; *"As iron sharpens iron, so one man sharpens another. As in water face reflects face, so the heart of man reflects man"*(AMP).

What's in your heart? What is going to be reflected in your actions, your attitudes, your character, and your speech?

Proverbs 27:9-10 tells us, *"The heartfelt counsel of a friend is as sweet as perfume and incense. Never abandon a friend—either yours or your fathers. When disaster strikes, you won't have to ask your brother for assistance. It is better to go to a neighbor than to a brother who lives far away."*

With men, something happens in the context of heart-to-heart fellowship. Hebrews 10:23-25 tells us; *"Let us hold tightly, without wavering to the hope we affirm, for God can be trusted to keep his promise. Let us think of ways to motivate one another to acts of love and good works. And let us not neglect our meeting together, as some people do, but encourage one another, especially now that the day of his return is drawing near."*

Men need other men to stimulate their soul's thirst for God. When men get together there is conversation about different subjects, but how many of those conversations revolve around what's happening in them spiritually. Are we asking each other the hard questions and being okay with being accountable to each other? How are you doing spiritually? Have you been reading your Bible? Have you been praying? What have you been reading lately, what have you been watching on TV? Have you been involved in or looking at material that is inappropriate? How about your mental thought life? What about your internet habits?

Find some men around you that you can trust and be completely honest and transparent with them. Ask each other the hard questions. Have a willingness to grow as a man in your spiritual life and be all you can be in your relationship with the Lord.

Every man desires to be a better man, a better husband, a better father, and a better follower of Jesus. On this Father's Day, I commend and say thank you for who you are, and your willingness to grow in your relationship with God and others.

Happy Father's Day and God Bless You.

♡ **Kay Murrell:** *I will miss Pastor Duane standing at the church door with a smile and pastoral greeting that always makes me feel so good. I am grateful for his* *prayers and being there for us; especially, in the last few years as my husband and I faced major health challenges. They both provided comfort and encouragement after Nolan's passing last summer. They adhere to preaching pure living according to the Word of God. Pastor Duane admires measuring everything according to God's Word regardless of what he or anyone else has said. Pastor Duane was fond of saying, "There is someone on the other side of your obedience." I have been on the other side of Pastor Duane and Gretchen's obedience as they have answered God's call on their life. I am immensely grateful for it. Love Kay Murrell*

CHAPTER 19

Importance of Missions

GOOD MORNING! EACH YEAR, FEBRUARY is the month that we focus on missions and the importance of being a missions "giving" and a missions "sending" church.

We read in Matthews 28:16-20, "*Then the eleven disciples left for Galilee, going to the mountain where Jesus had told them to go. When they saw him, they worshiped him—but some of them doubted! Jesus came and told his disciples, "I have been given all authority in heaven and on earth. Therefore, go and make disciples of all the nations, baptizing them in the name of the Father and the Son and the Holy Spirit. Teach these new disciples to obey all the commands I have given you. And be sure of this: I am with you always, even to the end of the age.""*

It is interesting that the word 'missionary' is not found in scripture. Yet when Jesus commanded His disciples to go into the world, He didn't use a big ad campaign, He didn't send out mailers, or buy billboard space to announce what He was going to do or how He was going to do it. He used people and He used those people in a variety of ways to spread His message.

So this morning we are going to move around a bit in the Scriptures and look at the Missions Mandate, The Missions Message, The Missions Method, and the Mission Field, as we look at the importance of missions in the church.

THE MISSIONS MANDATE (ACTS 1:8)

So, why are missions so important? We find the answer in Acts 1:8, "*But you will receive power when the Holy Spirit comes upon you. And you will be my witnesses, telling people about me everywhere—in Jerusalem, throughout Judea, in Samaria, and to the ends of the earth."*

The setting for this was at Jesus' Ascension on the Mount of Olives. There with His disciples, and Jesus gives them one last set of instructions in Acts 1:8, before ascending up into heaven. Notice Jesus tells the disciples gathered that they would receive power when the Holy Spirit had come upon them. The word power there is the Greek word 'dunamis' in the original language. We get our word 'dynamite' from it today.

Why does He want us to have that kind of power in our lives? We see the answer in the end of verse 8. We see that the disciples would be Jesus' witnesses in Jerusalem, Judea and Samaria, and to the ends of the earth.

But I want us to take note: It is only after they receive power from the Holy Spirit that they are called to be witnesses. The two go together. God's plan is that we have the Spirit before we step out into ministry. The two go together. Ministry without the Spirit is a miserable job.

Every one of us who know Christ, are called to be ministers. Not just me or our other church pastors. I stand up here and teach a message a couple of times a week. The real ministry happens when we leave this place. That is where the rubber meets the road.

Throughout history, studies show that most people are led to Christ by a friend or family member. You wouldn't think that is true, because most attention is paid to large crusades and outreaches by various ministries. But, for the most part, people come to a personal relationship with the Lord Jesus Christ through a personal relationship with another Christian.

Jesus told His followers in Matthew 28:19, *"Go therefore and make disciples of all the nations, baptizing them in the name of the Father and of the Son and of the Holy Spirit."* We call this the Great Commission. As Christians, this is our number one job, to express our faith by sharing it with others.

In Ephesians 4:12 it states, *"Their responsibility is to equip God's people to do his work and build up the church, the body of Christ."* Our mission here at Redmond Assembly of God is to equip the saints for the work of the ministry.

Our job is to equip you to minister and be a witness for Christ or as the NIV translation says, *"To equip his people for works of service, so that the body of Christ may be built up."*

So, why do I tie in Acts 1:8 with the Great Commission? Because at the same time it happened, Jesus was preparing His disciples for His departure. Acts 1:8 gives us some additional instructions as to how we accomplish that commission, the mandate from our Lord.

One thing I would like you to notice is the word 'witness' in Acts 1:8. It is the Greek word *martus*. We get our word *martyr* from it today. Today, we have that word, because many people, down through the years, have died for their faith. They died for their witness, many while away from home, trying to spread the gospel abroad.

Thousands of Christians had died for their witness that the word had taken on a new meaning – one who gave up their life for their faith.

How did all of these people have the courage and strength to face death because of their faith? The answer is simple – we have covered it at the beginning of verse 8. They had the power of the Holy Spirit within them. So, we have our mandate, what is the message?

THE MISSIONS MESSAGE (ACTS 20:20-21)

The Apostle Paul said, *"You know that I have not hesitated to preach anything that would be helpful to you but have taught you publicly and from house to house. I have declared to both Jews and Greeks that they must turn to God in repentance and have faith in our Lord Jesus"* (NIV).

I'm skipping a bit ahead of where we are at, but the setting for this verse is when Paul was headed back to Jerusalem for Pentecost, he sent for the Ephesian elders, and gave them some more instruction. He was simply recounting what he had done while he was there. He shared the gospel with them. The good news was a simple message – repent from your sins, and put your faith in – or follow, Jesus Christ."

The message is still the same today, and keep in mind that Paul was recounting what he was doing in Ephesus. The city of Ephesus was filled with idolatry and immorality. The culture was decayed and they were experiencing great problems.

Today we see people railing against sin. Sin is truly the affliction that affects all of us. Our sins will separate us from God for all eternity if we do not make the choice to follow Jesus as Paul is talking about here. But, if we make that decision, 1 John 1:9 tells us, *"If we confess our sins, He is faithful and just to forgive us our sins and to cleanse us from all unrighteousness"* (NKJV).

We need repentance. Repentance is turning away from our sins. Peter urged Simon the sorcerer to do this in the face of his blasphemy, asking to buy the power of the Holy Spirit, back in Acts Chapter 8.

But, if this had happened today, I would guess that Peter would get a "Hey, Pete! Take it easy on Simon. He's a new believer you know! Take it easy on him. Peter had the guts to share the truth in love even though it was probably a very tough thing to do.

Sin is an ugly thing, and it takes guts to make a stand against it; especially, in a foreign culture, where you don't fit in. Repentance is a necessary component in salvation though, along with faith in Jesus.

I certainly don't mean to sound harsh, but we all know people who have made a verbal commitment to Christ, and then they show up to church whenever it's convenient. They might even get involved with a ministry, and plug in and serve now and then.

To most anyone, even me as a pastor, it appears that this person is saved. Scripture tells us in 1 Samuel 16:7, *"…The Lord does not see as man sees; for man looks at the outward appearance, but the Lord looks at the heart"* (NKJV).

What is important here is what's in your heart. Simon had missed God by twelve inches. To some its' head knowledge not heart knowledge. There are also some churches that overemphasize the faith part, and lay low on the repentance. Other churches hit hard on the repentance, and get into legalism. They put the emphasis on the religion rather than the relationship, the faith part.

But, as Apostle Paul is telling us here in Acts Chapter 20, both are important, and I believe that it comes down to a balance, and if we tip the scales too far one way or another, we are in danger of misrepresenting the gospel.

If you boil it all down, the message of missions is the message of an evangelist – repent and believe. So, how does this get accomplished? We see this explained by the Apostle Paul himself, in Romans.

THE MISSIONS METHOD (ROMANS 10:13-15 NKJV)

For "whoever calls on the name of the Lord shall be saved." How then shall they call on Him in whom they have not believed? And how shall they believe in Him of whom they have not heard? And how shall they hear without a preacher? And how shall they preach unless they are sent? As it is written: "How beautiful are the feet of those who preach the gospel of peace, who bring glad tidings of good things!"

In this chapter, Paul is telling the Romans how the Jews rejected God by rejecting Jesus Christ. He then goes on to tell them that salvation is obtained by faith. Paul is telling the Romans simply this – faith comes about by the preaching of the gospel.

It is not just available to the Jewish nation, as some people would have them believe at that time. It wasn't a matter of religion and birthright; it was a matter of a relationship.

God could have chosen any means by which the message of salvation might have come (angelic messengers, direct working without a human preacher), but God's "normal" way of bringing people to Jesus Christ is through the preaching of the gospel.

God calls and raises up people to do His work on the earth. Evangelist Alan Redpath said that God could write the gospel in the stars if He chose to, but instead, He chose to use men, ordinary men, to carry His message to the ends of the earth.[1]

So no wonder those who preach the gospel of peace have beautiful feet; they are out partnering with God for the salvation of men.

That is the simple method of ministry for the missionary – to go where God has called them to go and carry the gospel message, and that message has dramatic results!

These two verses of scripture are the basis of why we send missionaries, and why we as a church support missionaries, and why we are here in

Redmond Oregon in the first place. Redmond Assembly of God is now over sixty-five years old and started here in this city so that people might hear the gospel and make a decision to follow Jesus Christ.

So, let's take a look at the mission field, in our final point.

THE MISSION FIELD (MATTHEW 28:18-20 NKJV)

Jesus came and spoke to them, saying, *"All authority has been given to Me in heaven and on earth. Go therefore and make disciples of all the nations, baptizing them in the name of the Father and of the Son and of the Holy Spirit, teaching them to observe all things that I have commanded you; and lo, I am with you always, even to the end of the age."* Amen.

To finish up, we are going to come back and look at Matthew's account of the great commission. The first thing I want us to notice is that the commission stems from the authority of Jesus Christ himself. All authority has been given to Him, as He is God. His commission to the disciples was to go and make more disciples, and as we have seen earlier, that happens by bringing the gospel to the people that need to hear it.

The message is clear – repent and believe. The commission is clear – GO! Go where? Jesus tells us this in verse 19 – to all nations. In Acts 1:8 , we get a little clearer view, when Jesus says, *"…And you will be my witnesses, telling people about me everywhere—in Jerusalem, throughout Judea, in Samaria, and to the ends of the earth."*

This is the mission field. God has given us this earthly planet to spread the gospel. While Jesus was traveling through Samaria, in the same journey where he confronted the woman at the well, we find Him saying this to His disciples:

"Do you not say, 'There are still four months and then comes the harvest'? Behold, I say to you, lift up your eyes and look at the fields, for they are already white for harvest! And he who reaps receives wages, and gathers fruit for eternal life, that both he who sows and he who reaps may rejoice together. For in this the saying is true: 'One sows and another reaps.' I sent you to reap that for which you have not labored; others have labored, and you have entered into their labors. And

many of the Samaritans of that city believed in Him because of the word of the woman who testified, "He told me all that I ever did" (John 4:35-39 NKJV).

The fields are white unto harvest. There are people out there literally dying to hear the gospel, and others that are dying to bring it to them, but the number taking the message is not enough. Many people, who live here in America, do not want to give up their lifestyle to go live in poverty on the mission field, but I praise Him for those who do.

To go to the mission field is a personal sacrifice, but the rewards are great. God blesses us in the local churches by giving us the opportunity to support and help missionaries while they are on the mission field.

James Hudson Taylor was a British Protestant Christian missionary to China and founder of the China Inland Mission. He died in China after spending 51 years sharing the gospel.[2]

While being a young missionary a man's question burned in Hudson Taylor's soul as he thought of the millions of Chinese who had never heard of Christ. The middle-aged man had long sought truth by studying Confucianism, Buddhism, and Taoism; but not until he heard the Gospel of Jesus did he find rest for his soul.

He eagerly testified to the Buddhists of the peace he had, and he began preaching Christ to his fellow countrymen. Shortly after his conversion he had asked Taylor how long the gospel had been known in England. When he was told it had been known for hundreds of years, the man was shocked. What! For hundreds of years you have had these glad tidings and only now have come to preach it to us? My father sought after the truth for more than twenty years, and died without finding it. Oh, why did you not come sooner?

It is my prayer, and I hope it would be yours too, that as we grow as a body here in Redmond, that we would continue to reach out by supporting missions work, not only for the masses of unbelievers in the world, but for us and our community as well.

And then he told them, "Go into all the world and preach the Good News to everyone.

— (Mark 16:15)

♥ **Susan Saadeddin**: *We are all so blessed to have had you as our pastor the last twenty-two years. Your kind, loving, and caring way of sharing the Word, touches my heart. I wish both you and Gretchen the best in retirement. May God bless you and your families as you enter the next season. We will miss you.* Susan Saadeddin

♥ **Rhonda Wagner**: *Thank you, Pastor Duane and Gretchen, for your precious and amazing loving kindness towards all of us. I will always be grateful to you both for your prayers and teachings. You both are a beautiful blessing and gift from Yeshua. May He bless you always!* Love Rhonda Wagner

CHAPTER 20

Christmas Story
of Salvation

MERRY CHRISTMAS TO ALL OF you! As I stand before you today, I would like to read from John 1:1-14 and it goes like this:

"In the beginning the Word already existed. The Word was with God, and the Word was God. He existed in the beginning with God. God created everything through him, and nothing was created except through him. The Word gave life to everything that was created, and his life brought light to everyone. The light shines in the darkness, and the darkness can never extinguish it.

God sent a man, John the Baptist, to tell about the light so that everyone might believe because of his testimony. John himself was not the light; he was simply a witness to tell about the light. The one who is the true light, who gives light to everyone, was coming into the world.

He came into the very world he created, but the world didn't recognize him. He came to his own people, and even they rejected him. But to all who believed him and accepted him, he gave the right to become children of God. They are reborn—not with a physical birth resulting from human passion or plan, but a birth that comes from God.

So the Word became human and made his home among us. He was full of unfailing love and faithfulness. And we have seen his glory, the glory of the Father's one and only Son."

I would to tell you a story. A man stood at a metro station in Washington DC and started to play the violin; it was a cold January morning in 2007. He played six Bach pieces for about forty-five minutes. During that time, since it was rush hour, it was calculated that over one thousand people went through the station, most of them on their way to work. Three minutes went by and a middle-aged man noticed there was a musician playing. He slowed his pace and stopped for a few seconds and then hurried up to meet his schedule. A minute later, the violinist received his first dollar tip: A woman threw the money in his case and without stopping continued to walk.

A few minutes later, someone leaned against the wall to listen to him, but the man listened for a few minutes and then went on his way.

The one who paid the most attention was a three year old boy. His mother tagged him along, hurried but the boy stopped to look at the violinist. Finally, the mother pushed hard and the child continued to walk turning his head the whole time. This action was repeated by several other children. All the parents, without exception, forced them to move on, in the forty-five minutes the musician played, only six people stopped and stayed awhile to listen.

About twenty people gave him money, but continued to walk at their normal pace. He collected $32.17. When he finished playing and silence took over, no one noticed it. No one applauded, nor was there any recognition. No one knew, but this violinist was Joshua Bell, one of the best musicians in the world. He played one of the most intricate pieces ever written on a violin worth 3.5 million dollars.

Two days before playing in the subway, Joshua Bell sold out a theater in Boston with the average seats selling for $100 each. This is a real story. Joshua Bell playing incognito in the metro subway station was organized by the Washington Post as part of a social experiment about perception, taste, and the priorities of people.

What were the take a ways for the experiment?

In a common place environment at an inappropriate hour: Do we perceive beauty? Do we stop to appreciate it? Do we recognize the talent in an unexpected context? If we do not have a moment to stop and listen to one of the best musicians in the world playing some of the greatest music every written, how many other things are we missing? (Gene Weingarten, Washington Post, October 14, 2014)[1]

This morning I want us to pause for a moment to celebrate the glory of Heaven ringing out loudly, proclaiming the wonder of God in the world; Christ Jesus came into the world to offer redemption and lasting hope; He is the King of Kings!

It is in Christ we hear the bells of Heaven ringing loudly. It is in Christ we see God, the grand violinist, as it were, playing a sweet melody of hope and eternal life, and redemption. We have been invited by God this morning to attend this wonderful symphony called life. We have been ushered into our seats by the Holy Spirit and here we are overwhelmed by the majesty and beauty of the song being played; Emmanuel—God within us!

Listen to the words again this morning; *"He came into the very world he created, but the world didn't recognize him. He came to his own people, and even they rejected him. But to all who believed him and accepted him, he gave the right to become children of God. They are reborn—not with a physical birth resulting from human passion or plan, but a birth that comes from God"* (John 1:10-13).

This morning we celebrate not the birth of just some wise man, not just a great teacher, and certainly not simply just another prophet of God. We celebrate the coming of God in the flesh, the promised Messiah, the Christ Child who came into this world to save this world.

It is Christ Jesus who came into the world to set captives free, and to offer the hope of eternal salvation to you and to me. Of all of the sounds of the unwrapping of paper from the gifts that we will receive this season, as you listen to them, let's hear an even greater sound, the sound of the unwrapping and the unveiling of Jesus Christ to the world.

Let us take a moment to slow down and stop, even as you have this morning, to listen for the sound of salvation, the ringing of the bells of Grace, ringing in the wonder and the beauty and the majesty of Christ Jesus who was given to us. In Isaiah 9:6 it says, "For a child is born to us, a son is given to us. The government will rest on his shoulders. And he will be called Wonderful Counselor, Mighty God, Everlasting Father, Prince of Peace."

Pastor Rick Warren describes what salvation means:[2]

Jesus came to rescue us. We can't solve all of our problems on our own. Without Jesus we are trapped in the expectations of others. We are trapped in living for the approval of our peers. We are trapped in our addictions. We have tried to change over and over again, but we don't have the needed power to escape. Jesus came to give us that power.

Jesus came to recover us. We all long to recover parts of our lives that have been lost. Without Christ, we long to recover our strength, our confidence, our reputations, our innocence, and our relationship with God. Only Jesus can do that.

Jesus came to reconnect us. Many people think that God will scold them if they come back to him. But God isn't mad at you. He is mad *about* you. Jesus came to Earth on the first Christmas to reconcile us to God, to give us harmony with him again.

Jesus came to Earth to give us the gift of himself. Too many of us celebrate his birthday without accepting this free gift of salvation. It goes unwrapped year after year after year.

You were made by God and for God. Until you and I understand that, life will never make sense.

This Christmas, open up the most *important* gift you've been given: a new relationship with God through Jesus Christ his Son.

♥ **Chris and Kathy Walter:** Duane and Gretchen, we have always appreciated your servant's heart. You've always been willing to do things with others or come alongside and help. Not only did our church benefit from that, but other churches also benefited. Through your ministry, you've touched count-less lives, known and unknown. When God calls us forward to receive our reward, yours is going to be exceptional.

When you moved to Redmond, we decided we wanted to get to know our new pastor and family on a personal level. We were so pleased to find com-monalities and a great friendship! We have shared and prayed for each other. Watching our children grow and marry, praying for God's blessings. We've heard troubling health news and watched parents transition to heaven. An essential part of our friendship is that we have enjoyed much laughter together and shared a lot of food and games.

I remember our first camping trip. Cooking fried chicken, and Chris and Duane trying to split a piece of firewood with a screwdriver. Laughing, that didn't work out so well. Hope we get to do some more of that. Duane, I'm still sorry you banged your head on the short doorway after lights out because I talked you into doing a narration for the singing Christmas Tree. Thanks for your support and participation. We love you guys. Friends for life! Chris and Kathy Walter

Delores Beadnell: I have only been attending Redmond Assembly for six months and I love Pastor Duane's talks. I am going to miss hearing him speak to us about God. I wish both Pastor and Gretchen a great retirement and hopefully, we will get to see them on occasion.

CHAPTER 21

A Heavenly Place

YOU ARE CHERISHED. YOU ARE chosen. You are called by the hope of heaven to an intimate, life-giving relationship with Jesus. Are you hearing His voice? Are you living in His love throughout each day? As you take a few minutes each day to tune your ear to heaven's voice, pray that you will come to know how deeply and personally Jesus loves you. Pray that you hear from the One who knows you by name.

As believers, we celebrate as our loved ones go home to be with the Lord. We cherish the memories we have with them; we miss their presence and their love as we grieve our loss. For Jesus Christ, this is a time of gladness and joy, and great celebration that your loved one is in their heavenly home with Him.

2 Corinthians 5:6-8 tells us; *"So we are always confident, even though we know that as long as we live in these bodies we are not at home with the Lord. That is why we live by believing and not by seeing. Yes, we are fully confident, and we would rather be away from these earthly bodies, for then we will be at home with the Lord."*

For a believer there is no greater joy than to be in the presence of the One who loves them like no one else ever could. We celebrate the life of the Christian. When they die and go to heaven, it is really a day of celebration; it is not a day of regret, but truly a day of rejoicing. We come together to rejoice and celebrate our loved ones life. We come together to remember special moments that we had together here on earth.

Those loved ones who have a relationship with Jesus Christ know of the wonderful "promises" that we find in Chapter 14 of John. I would like to share these with you.

In John 14:1-6 it states, *"Don't let your hearts be troubled. Trust in God, and trust also in me. ²There is more than enough room in my Father's home. If this were not so, would I have told you that I am going to prepare a place for you? ³When everything is ready, I will come and get you, so that you will always be with me where I am. ⁴And you know the way to where I am going." ⁵"No, we don't know, Lord," Thomas said. "We have no idea where you are going, so how can we know the way?" ⁶Jesus told him, "I am the way, the truth, and the life. No one can come to the Father except through me.""*

The first promise to those who put their trust in Christ Jesus is that we don't have to fear death. Jesus said; "Don't let your hearts be troubled" (John 14:1).

We are troubled when we don't know what is going to happen when we die, but Jesus has taken the fear out of dying. Jesus has conquered the grave and death so there doesn't need to be any fear about our eternal future.

Revelation 1:17-18 tells us; *"...Don't be afraid! I am the First and the Last. I am the living one who died. Look, I am alive forever and ever! And I hold the keys of death and the grave."*

Do you know what the good news is today? Death had no hold on Jesus nor does it have a hold on us. Because Jesus conquered death there should be no fear for the Christian because through Christ Jesus we also conquer death. We are troubled when we view death as an end instead of a beginning.

2 Corinthians 5:1 tells us; *"For we know that when this earthly tent we live in is taken down—when we die and leave these earthly bodies—we will have a home in heaven, an eternal body made for us by God himself and not by human hands."*

When a person passes on, they shed the temporary for the eternal, the tarnished for the spotless and the passing for the everlasting. Yes our earthly bodies die, however our heavenly bodies endure for all eternity.

The second promise Jesus gave us to those who put their trust in Him is that, He is preparing a place for "them" in Heaven. What has he prepared? I love to read this scripture.

Revelation 21:4 tells us; *"He will wipe every tear from their eyes, and there will be no more death or sorrow or crying or pain. All these things are gone forever."*

Heaven is a place with no more sorrow or crying. It is a place where the hurts and disappointments of this world will have no more sting. It is a place where the frustrations of life are replaced with unspeakable joy. It is a place where the pains of life are not permitted and the failures of life control us no longer.

Heaven is a place with no more pain. Heaven has no handicap parking places, no pharmacies and no prescriptions to fill. Heaven doesn't have hospitals, nursing homes, or rehabilitation centers. In Heaven, Jesus will gently touch your face, wipe away your tears, and make all things new.

Heaven is a place of great beauty! Let's look at a glimpse of what Heaven will be like when we arrive.

The Bible states in Revelation 21:18-27, *"The wall was made of jasper, and the city was pure gold, as clear as glass. The wall of the city was built on foundation stones inlaid with twelve gems: the first was jasper, the second sapphire, the third agate, the fourth emerald, the fifth onyx, the sixth carnelian, the seventh chrysolite, the eighth beryl, the ninth topaz, the tenth chrysoprase, the eleventh jacinth, the twelfth amethyst. The twelve gates were made of pearls — each gate from a single pearl! And the main street was pure gold, as clear as glass. No temple could be seen in the city, for the Lord God Almighty and the Lamb are its temple. And the city has no need of sun or moon, for the glory of God illuminates the city, and the Lamb is its light. The nations of the earth will walk in its light, and the rulers of the world will come and bring their glory to it. Its' gates never close at the end of day because there is no night. And all the nations will bring their glory and honor into the city. Nothing evil will be allowed to enter — no one who practices shameful idolatry and dishonesty — but only those whose names are written in the Lamb's Book of Life."*

Revelation 22:1-5 tell us, *"And the angel showed me a pure river with the water of life, clear as crystal, flowing from the throne of God and of the Lamb, coursing down the center of the main street. On each side of the river grew a tree of life, bearing twelve crops of fruit, with a fresh crop each month. The leaves were used for medicine to heal the nations. No longer will anything be cursed. For the throne of God and of the Lamb will be there, and his servants will worship him. And they will see his face, and his name will be written on their foreheads. And there will be no night there — no need for lamps or sun — for the Lord God will shine on them. And they will reign forever and ever."*

The third promise found in John 14:3 is that Jesus himself *personally receives us.*
Jesus receives us with open arms. In John 14:3, Jesus says, "When everything is ready, I will come and get you, so that you will always be with me where I am." He receives us with a love we could never know and fully understand until we see him face to face. It is a love that mends every hurt, understands every feeling, and completely satisfies every longing of our soul.

The last promise is that there is only one way to enter heaven.
Jesus, in John 14:4-6 (paraphrase), says to Apostle Thomas, "Thomas you say you don't know the way to heaven but you do, I am the way, the truth, and the life."

As a Christian, this is what we know and understand. A person without a relationship with Jesus has no hope of Heaven. Jesus came to take away the sins of the world. Christians believe the greatest promise ever given, and it is for everyone, the promise God made by sending Jesus, His only Son, into the world.

John 3:16-18 *"For God so loved the world that he gave his one and only Son, that whoever believes in him shall not perish but have eternal life. For God did not send his Son into the world to condemn the world, but to save the world through him. Whoever believes in him is not condemned, but whoever does not believe stands condemned already because they have not believed in the name of God's one and only Son"* (NIV).

People who believe and live their life around this promise with a relationship with Jesus, will experience a Heaven that is unimaginable and experience a love that is incomprehensible.

As a pastor, I want everyone to have that same relationship with the Savior. I want everyone to be in Heaven when they die. God's promise is through the following scriptures:

First you have already heard Jesus say; "I am the way, the truth and the life. No man comes to the Father except through me" (John 14:6). There is no other way to enter Heaven, it is only through a personal relationship with Jesus Christ. It doesn't have to do with religion, it doesn't have to do with what church you attend, it doesn't have to do whether you are a good person or not.

1 John 5:11 tells us; *"And this is what God has testified: He has given us eternal life, and this life is in his Son. So whoever has God's Son has life; whoever does not have his Son does not have life. I have written this to you who believe in the Son of God, so that you may know you have eternal life".*

Romans 10:9-11 states, *"That if you confess with your mouth the Lord Jesus and believe in your heart that God has raised Him from the dead, you will be saved. [10]For with the heart one believes unto righteousness, and with the mouth confession is made unto salvation. [11]For the Scripture says, "Whoever believes on Him will not be put to shame"* (NKJV).

1 John 1:8-10 says, *"If we claim we have no sin, we are only fooling ourselves and not living in the truth. But if we confess our sins to him, he is faithful and just to forgive us our sins and to cleanse us from all wickedness. If we claim we have not sinned, we are calling God a liar and showing that his word has no place in our hearts."*

2 Corinthians 5:17 states, *"This means that anyone who belongs to Christ has become a new person. The old life is gone; a new life has begun."*

In prayer: Our Gracious Heavenly Father, we once again thank you for the blessings of our loved ones who pass from earth to your heavenly place. We thank you for all the lives each person has touched and the memories that they have left us. And now Father, we ask that you comfort the family members and friends that have been left behind to grieve. Help us to always remember the frailty of life. For it is in the precious name of Jesus we pray. Amen

♡ **Kristy Lane**: Thank you for your many appreciated years of faithful devotion, God-centered wisdom, loving dedication, and faithful example of living out the Word. You have reached many hearts and souls to live for Christ, exemplifying putting God first, honoring Him always, and listening to the Holy Spirit's guidance, promptings, and discernment. We love your humble, good-natured humor, kind/loving heart, and sincere character as you have shared the life experiences God has given you that has led and convicted us to a deeper relationship with Christ. Well done, good and faithful servant, for blessing our church abundantly with His grace, love, and powerful messages of what He wants the church to know. You will be missed! May you both have abundant joy, peace, contentment, and good health in retirement as God blesses you for continually showing Jesus' love to others. With much love and blessings in Him. Kristy Lane

CHAPTER 22

On The Journey Home

IN CONCLUSION, AS AN AUTHOR, I would like to say, "We are all *On the Journey….Home.*" Pastor Duane and Gretchen are going home to happily retire on their mini-farm. Our Lord will still use them as a vessel to convey the love He has for everyone.

After months of interviewing Pastor Duane and Gretchen, writing up his sermons, and receiving the congregation's wonderful comments, I experienced the Lord reaching out to me to deliver a message.

I was getting ready to go to dinner at our friends, Jerry and Donna's home. I was standing in the bathroom brushing my teeth and drying my hair. I wasn't thinking about anything, except getting ready. Out of the blue, a strong voice by my right ear, said, *"Thank you Susan for following Me; thank you for **honoring** Duane & Gretchen by writing this book, because "they don't understand" how much I love them and appreciate their service."* At the time, I was bewildered and taken back. Where did that come from? For one thing, I don't thank myself for doing anything, and two, the words, "they don't understand" struck me as odd. Of course, they understand that God loves them. They are pastors and in the ministry

Pastor Duane and Gretchen have always said, "our life is not worthy of a book, we are just ordinary folks, trying to get by in life, doing the same thing everybody else does." They are humble to the core and that is why we all love them. They are 'real', honest, transparent people, who happen to love God with all their heart, mind, and soul. They love and support their flock with an undying love, an unconditional love, and a love we can strive for, as we love others. They have said over and over in the interviews, "we didn't have an exceptional life, we are just ordinary people; a book about us would be about ten pages. (Laughter)

I realized that God had a message for me to give them. A message that is conveyed in this book over and over and it comes from the love of the people of this congregation, which comes from Jesus. And, I also believe with all my heart, God wanted them to know how much He loves them and appreciates their service to Him.

As individuals we each have a life that is uniquely planned out by God. As we follow Jesus, we relax and listen to His gentle voice and try to make good decisions. When we are young, we make decisions based on what is going on in society or based on what we have learned in childhood. We want to fit into the world and be accepted. When we are called by Jesus, we attempt to follow and learn what He wants us to do. Through trial and error and making some mistakes, we feel God's continual gentle love pull on us. We struggle as we go through unbearable trials. God has a way of pulling on our heart strings as He strengthens us, builds our character, and makes us one of His disciples.

He doesn't force us to believe in Him; we have free will to turn to Him and love Him. When we commit our lives to Jesus, we yield and surrender to Him as we die to ourselves, and we ask for forgiveness as we repent of our wrong doing. We accept Him into our lives and we are 'born again' to a life in Jesus. We spend the rest of our lives in sanctification, where Jesus molds and shapes us for eternity.

God uses ordinary folks to do extraordinary things for Him. The Lord seeks humble people who hunger and thirst for Him to be used as His servants. Pastor Duane and Gretchen happen to be chosen by God, long before they were knitted in the womb, to be in church ministry. As noted, earlier in their story, Pastor Duane walked away from the Lord for six years as a teenager and young adult, but the Lord had other plans. He tortured him with the vision that he had missed the rapture. What a strong statement the Lord made to pull him close to Him!

When Duane returned to his walk with the Lord, he felt all the shame and guilt disappear. He was hungry and thirsty to learn more, and he followed what the Lord wanted him to do. Has it always been easy? No, like most of us, life's trials bring them to their knees as they keep their eyes on Jesus during the years of battling leukemia and receiving treatments to maintain life. In 2018, losing so many loved ones in our congregation, and then tragically losing a young granddaughter last year they show us the real, human-side of grief and sorrow.

Through all the years of ministry, they keep their chin up and looking to the Lord for answers, taking it one step at a time, making the best of each day. Gretchen mentions, "Each day is so precious because you never know when the Lord will call each of us home." Having a positive attitude toward life, regardless of what you are going through, tells the Lord you trust Him, which means you believe in Him, and praise Him for what He will do.

We all have those days where we need to sit, drink coffee, pet our dog, and stare into the campfire. The peace of Jesus is always available to us, no matter what we are going through. Jesus needed those quiet times too. He would leave and go across the lake or into the wilderness to be alone, pray, and talk to His Father. Jesus showed us how to be 'real' too.

As a writer putting this book together, I want to personally thank Pastor Duane and Gretchen for sharing their story and trusting me to write their words. My heart has been changed knowing the difficulty of sharing the vulnerable parts of their lives with another. I want to thank God for 'nudging' me to write and honor their service to Him.

I felt the love and respect people have for Pastor Duane and Gretchen. The staff expressed how they were supported in growing in the ministry. The word "family" and "mentor" were used to define their relationships. As part of the congregation, many people submitted their comments and each one resonated with their hearts and their love for them. Surprisingly, many have been friends for twenty years or more, and others had been through very difficult trials such as losing a loved one, medical conditions, or family issues. Pastor Duane and Gretchen walked alongside them grieving with them. Pastor Duane's has always said, "We are family and I love all of you".

This book, 'On the Journey…Home' is Pastor's way of saying, we are all on the journey of life with all the work and play, ups and downs, happy times and difficult times, but eventually, as Believers, we are all led to Heaven when the Lord calls us **Home** to spend eternity with Him.

Thank you Pastor Duane and Gretchen for leading and loving your congregation, as you taught us about the Lord's love. We are all thankful to have been part of your flock. You both are the "full meal deal"!

As you retire, after forty-one years of ministry, the Lord is 'indeed' pleased.

♡ **Bob and Susan Free**: This book may end, but your 'gas tanks' are full of life as you head towards retirement. May you find sacred rest, peacefulness, laughter and joy in the years ahead. You are surrounded by love from your family, friends, and Jesus, and a few cows and dogs. Someday, we will all meet again, maybe over cinnamon rolls and coffee. We love you! Bob & Susan Free

Pastor Duane & Gretchen Pippitt

They served the Lord forty-one years in ministry in Salem, Silverton, and Redmond, Oregon for the Assembly of God churches.

Retirement: August 31, 2024

Pippitt Mini Cattle Ranch

Established in 1979, the year they were married. They have two lab dogs, Gus and Mac, three stray cats, cattle, and the neighbor's emus and pet pig visit often.

Pastor Duane's favorite animals are "cows," and he loves raising them for beef dinners (Ginger beef, Salisbury Sally, Ribeye Rosy, and Juicy Lucy). They also donate to the church's local food bank.

This is a beautiful farm country for relaxing, visiting, and watching the sunsets. On sunny days, you can see Mt. Jefferson in the background.

This is a water canal that irrigates their land during the summer for growing hay for the cattle. They both look forward to working the fields and sitting by the campfire in their backyard.

Gretchen and the neighbor's friendly emus. They love to be petted and be fed fun treats.

*Duane's bright red 1965 Chevy El Camino that he and his
87 year old Dad installed a new motor in.*

*Gretchen and Duane standing in the field up the hill from their home
(located in background on lower right). Duane has his own irrigation
and farm equipment and plans to grow hay, cut and bale it,
and store it for his cows.*

Sitting by the campfire...Ahhh!

O God, You have taught me from my earliest childhood,
and I constantly tell others about the wonderful things You do.
Now I am old and gray,
do not abandon me, O God,
Let me proclaim Your power to this new generation,
Your mighty miracles to all who come after me.

Psalms 71:17-18

For all who have entered into God's rest have rested from their labors,
just as God did after creating the world.

Hebrews 4:10

"What's more, I am with you, and I will protect you wherever you go.
One day I will bring you back to this land.
I will not leave you until I have finished giving you
everything I have promised you."

Genesis 28:15

LORD'S PRAYER

"But you, when you pray, go into your room, and when you have shut your door, pray to your Father who *is* in the secret *place;* and your Father who sees in secret will reward you openly. And when you pray, do not use vain repetitions as the heathens *do.* For they think that they will be heard for their many words. Therefore do not be like them. For your Father knows the things you have need of before you ask Him" (Matthew 6:6-9 NKJV).

In this manner, therefore, pray:

Our Father in heaven
Hallowed be Your name.
Your kingdom come
Your will be done
On earth as *it is* in heaven.
Give us this day our daily bread.
And forgive us our debts,
As we forgive our debtors.
And do not lead us into temptation,
But deliver us from the evil one.
For Yours is the kingdom and the power and the glory forever. Amen.

— (Matthew 6:9-13 NKJV)

CELEBRATE RECOVERY©

Celebrate Recovery is a safe place to find community and freedom from the painful issues that are controlling our lives. This program is a Christ-centered, twelve-step recovery program for anyone struggling with any kind of hurt, hang-up, or habit that affects their desire to have a better life.

This program started in 1991 at Saddleback Church in Lake Forest, California. John Baker wrote Pastor Rick Warren the "now-famous, concise, 13-page single-spaced" letter outlining the vision God had given John for Celebrate Recovery.

The first night forty-three people attended, and Celebrate Recovery was born. Today, there are now thirty-five thousand churches participating around the world, and that number continues to grow. To date, over five million individuals have completed a Step Study, nine-week study course. This is a program that brings the healing power of Jesus Christ to the hurting and broken through Celebrate Recovery's Step Studies, The Journey Begins, and The Journey Continues.

In addition, Celebrate Recovery is growing in recovery houses, rescue missions, universities, and prisons around the world. This is an exciting and growing outreach opportunity for Celebrate Recovery. We are a part of something much larger than one church's Celebrate Recovery. We are part of a movement that God is blessing.

The Celebrate Recovery program has about 25 percent alcohol and chemical/drug dependency participants. The other 75 percent have hurts, hang-ups, and habits that may include sexual and physical abuse, mental and emotional abuse, codependency, the death of a loved one(s), the murder of a family member, depression, anxiety, divorce, eating disorders, separation from children, job anxiety, or a medical condition or illness. The list goes on to include any hurt, hang-up, or habit that a person may be suffering from, sometimes in silence, in their life.

Imagine a safe environment where people accept you just the way you are and love you through your pain. The goal is to gently identify the main core issues why you medicate or why you hurt. In doing so, you get down to the root cause of your hurt with the "who, what, why, how it made you react, and the outcome." This helps each person to move through to a point of managing the pain. It can be lifesaving. Jesus Christ is the great Healer.

Life has a way of changing by just a simple phone call in which you hear "that your child died in a car accident"; that "you have terminal cancer"; that "your sister was found murdered"; or that "your husband wants a divorce." All the situations we face in life have an effect on us, some that can change our lifestyles forever. People can harbor bitterness or un-forgiveness for years and not know this is affecting them. They just know they feel angry, depressed, resentful, and unhappy with life.

If you find yourself in a place of hurts, hang-ups, and habits that are making your life unmanageable, contact the nearest Celebrate Recovery group or go online to www.celebraterecovery.com for more information. Once you ask Christ into your heart as your Lord and Savior, true healing and recovery can begin. This freedom creates peace, serenity, joy, and most importantly, a relationship with Jesus.

Help is available today: 1-800-273-8255
Emergency 911
Suicide & Crisis Lifeline 988
Website: www.celebraterecovery.com

<u>Local Chapter</u>
Tuesday Nights: 7:00-8:30pm
Tuesday nights are a time of worship with a lesson or testimony, followed by small groups.

Redmond Assembly of God
1865 W Antler Avenue
Redmond, OR 97756

Mike and Deborah Cook, Ministry Leaders (541) 647-3333
Sharon Weldin, Lead State Representative and West X-Factor (541) 325-3853
www.facebook.com/celebraterecoveryredmondoregon

END NOTES

Introduction:

1. https://blog.coldwellbanker.com/the-origin-and-true-meaning-of-home/

Chapter 4 - Grief Stricken

1. Dunn, Bill and Leonard, Kathy, *Through a Season of Grief*, Devotional Daily, April 13, 2024.
2. Dr. David Jeremiah, the pastor of Shadow Mountain Church in California, writes in his bestselling book, *God Has Not Forgotten You*
3. Ibid
4. Dr. Earl McQuay, a minister who lost a son in a tragic car accident, wrote a small book entitled *Beyond Eagles: A Father's Grief and Hope.*

Chapter 9 – Commitment to God

1. Hokey Pokey song lyrics: https://www.learningstationmusic.com/blog/2014/02/05/hokey-pokey-lyrics/
2. John Blanchard, comp., More Gathered Gold, Welwyn, Hertfordshire, England: Evangelical Press, 1984, p. 344.
3. James A. Pike, Beyond Anxiety, 1953. Cited in The Treasury of Religious and Spiritual Quotations: Words to Live By, Rebecca Davis and Susan Mesner, Eds., Pleasantville: Reader's Digest, 1994, p. 638

Chapter 11 - Understanding Contentment

1. Holman Illustrated Bible Dictionary, 2003 Holman Bible Publishers, Contentment, page 335

Chapter 13 - Facing Impossible Situations

1. Evans, Tony, Book of Illustrations: Stories, Quotes, and Anecdotes from More Than 30 Years of Preaching and Public Speaking, Moody Publishers 2009

Chapter 14 – Cultivating Thankfulness

1. Barclay, William, Daily Study Bible, https://www.gotquestions.org/William-Barclay.html
2. 2015 Robert Emmons, professor of psychology at the University of California in Davis
3. Lauren Dunn, "Be thankful: Science says gratitude is good for your health," in "Today," November 26, 2015

Chapter 17- Mother's Day – Empowering with Encouragement

1. William Arthur Ward Quote, https://www.brainyquote.com/authors/william-arthur-ward-quotes

Chapter 18 – Father's Day Message

1. White, Jerry, *Dangers Men Face*,
2. Obid
3. L. Sweet,The Jesus Prescription for a Healthy Life, p. 152

Chapter 19 Importance of Missions

1. Redpath, Alan https://en.wikipedia.org/wiki/Alan_Redpath
2. James Hudson Taylor, Chinese Missionary, https://en.wikipedia.org/wiki/Hudson_Taylor

Chapter 20 Christmas Story of Salvation

1. Gene Weingarten, Washington Post, October 14, 2014)
2. Rick Warren, https://pastorrick.com/devotional/english/full-post/ what-salvation-means-for-you
3. December 2017

ABOUT THE AUTHOR

Susan Free has spent thirty-two years teaching classes on psychology, relationships, and various Bible studies, primarily in women's ministries. She has also taught community education classes at Portland Community College in subjects regarding psychology and real estate. In the past, she also served as a grief and stepfamily counselor.

A native Oregonian, Susan enjoys writing, teaching, hiking in the Cascade Mountains, camping, and spending time with family and friends. She and her husband, Robert, have four daughters and four grandchildren and enjoy a quiet life in Redmond, Oregon.

Susan received a Bachelor of Arts degree in psychology/social science from Marylhurst University in West Linn, Oregon.

Other books written by Susan Free:

Forgiving the KILLER while Grieving Uriah,

Available through Amazon, Barnes & Noble, Walmart, and other book outlets.

Published by Trilogy Christian Publishing, a wholly subsidiary of TBN – June 2024.

https://www.amazon.com/Forgiving-Killer-While-Grieving-Uriah/dp/B0D4MRMLWF

Ready or Not, The Lord Is Coming,
Available through Amazon and Barnes & Noble.

https://www.amazon.com/Ready-Lord-Coming-Susan-Free-ebook/dp/B0126NP9L8

FREE THE HEART
MINISTRIES
"Comfort and Healing"

For more information about ordering additional books or reading blogs on grief and forgiveness, visit our website at: http://www.freetheheartministries.com. Contact author for free newsletter at email: freetheheartministries@gmail.com.

Made in the USA
Middletown, DE
29 July 2024

58078406R00113